DIRECT PATH TO THE
CFA® CHARTER

DIRECT PATH TO THE
CFA® CHARTER

Savvy, Proven Strategies for Passing Your
Chartered Financial Analyst® Exams

RACHEL BRYANT, CFA

Published by Intellitwist, LLC

Intellitwist LLC

ISBN: 978-1-941074-01-5

Library of Congress Control Number: 2013923801
Printed in the United States of America

"A straight path never leads anywhere except to the objective."

–Andre Gide

CONTENTS

Acknowledgements   *ix*

Preface   *xi*

Part One: Answers to Big Questions   1

Chapter 1   CFA Program Overview   3

Chapter 2   Does Industry Experience Matter?   19

Chapter 3   The First Secret to Passing CFA Exams   29

Chapter 4   The Second Secret to Passing CFA Exams   41

Chapter 5   What Ethics Is Really All About   53

Chapter 6   A Quiet, Important Statistic   67

Part Two: Study Regimen   81

Chapter 7   The 300-Hour Trap   83

Chapter 8   A Study Plan from Start to Finish   97

Chapter 9   Curriculum Books or Study Notes?   111

Chapter 10   The Power of Flashcards   125

Chapter 11   Transforming Knowledge into Test Performance   133

Contents

Chapter 12   A Differentiating Practice Test Strategy   145

Chapter 13   Study Groups Are Overrated   155

Chapter 14   Read This When You Want to Quit   163

Chapter 15   Test Day Suggestions   169

Chapter 16   Putting It All Together   183

Final Thoughts   *193*

Level I, II, and III Recap and Sample Schedules   *197*

Test Preparation Resources   *215*

About the Author   *219*

References   *221*

ACKNOWLEDGEMENTS

Thank you to my incredible family and friends who supported me through the CFA Program and again as I wrote a book about it. You've shown impressive patience in putting up with me.

To my editors, sounding boards, and late-night advisors, your selfless dedication and belief in this book show through on every page. You didn't just help shape the book; you shaped me, too. Thank you.

To the CFA charterholders who gave their input and words of encouragement, thank you for helping me to write the book that we wish we had when we were in the CFA Program. To the candidates, thank you for asking fantastic questions and being hungry for answers; your enthusiasm, determination, and strength are truly inspiring.

And, to my husband, Darby ... because of your support and sacrifices, I have the rare and wonderful experience of pursuing my dreams. This book and my CFA charter are as much yours as they are mine; I couldn't have done either without you. Thank you.

PREFACE

You want to pass the Chartered Financial Analyst® exams, and do so on the first try. Helping you achieve both goals is my consistent, unwavering focus throughout the following chapters. There is a direct path to the CFA® charter; it involves strategy, foresight, adaptability, and a willingness to step outside the normal, average routine. With the right preparation, you can become a CFA charterholder in a timeframe that fits your career track. I will guide you through this tough and rewarding journey.

By picking up this book, you've already demonstrated commitment. However, you also need to know how to pass exams that fail roughly 60% of all challengers at every Level and greater than 90% overall.[1] You're looking for clarity. Plain and simple.

You've got the drive, but reliable information and guidance would be nice. I know how you feel. I understand your anxiety, confusion, and excitement in beginning this process; I've been there, staring at my newly arrived study materials, wondering if my plan for tackling them would work. But, my plan did work. I passed every Level of the CFA Program on my first try with scores that outperformed. Let me be clear: I am no genius. It was my study plan, which I honed throughout the CFA Program, that produced these results. With this book, you have the benefit of my retrospective insight before taking the exam.

Even with a sound study plan, there are things that I wish I'd known before I started the CFA Program; this book shares those findings. I aim to support, encourage, and guide you through all phases of the CFA Program and help you to convert your candidate status to that of a CFA charterholder. You deserve to know up front what this program is about and how to succeed in it. Keep an open mind and seriously consider my suggestions. I had to figure it out as I went along. You don't have to.

This book empowers you with answers. Over the course of two sections—(1) "Answers to Big Questions" and (2) "Study Regimen"—every chapter focuses on getting you a passing score on your Level's exam the first time. To serve this objective, each chapter concludes with a list of key takeaways that can be quickly referenced in the future. With these key takeaways, you can easily refer back as you move through the Levels.

This book is not about generalities. I provide specific, actionable strategies and explain exactly how to implement them in a way that can make a considerable difference in your exam results. In every chapter, there are valuable insights for all three CFA Levels. At the end of the book, I provide a summary of strategies for each Level with sample study schedules. These will help you to execute a study plan in every stage of the CFA Program.

I can't promise a pain-free journey. There are no short cuts that can miraculously deliver passing results with little or no effort. There will be long study sessions, sleepless nights, and never-ending piles of flashcards. What I can promise is a journey free of *unnecessary* pain. You don't want to overly pad your performance on what are, in the end, pass/fail tests. You don't need to waste time striving for an "A," though barely passing is a dangerous game, too. I will constantly straddle this line, laying out what you need to do to pass comfortably without burdening you with extra labor that adds little value.

I'll treat you like the adult you are and not turn away from the fact that failure is a possibility. Lots of people fail. Over one million people have taken the tests in the last decade alone, while only about 150,000 CFA charters have been awarded globally since 1963.[2] Many fail while few pass.

One of the most pervasive CFA Program myths is that failing candidates simply don't study hard enough. This is true for a small number but, in reality, most candidates study hard. More commonly, candidates fail because they study for a career in finance instead of a passing score on the CFA tests. There's a difference. **You must have a study regimen that is focused on passing the tests, not simply learning the material.** That is what this book is all about; you want to learn, and you also want to pass.

You probably don't have to be told that this program is going to be difficult because you've heard of the Program's low passing rates, you know that smart people fail every year, and you're wondering how you can avoid that fate. You need to know the things that make a difference.

So, what truly determines performance in the CFA Program? It's about understanding the inner workings of the Program and how to adjust to its dynamics. It's about recognizing the nuances of each Level and tailoring your approach to fit the one at hand. It's about preparing in an above-average way, since only above-average performance gets a passing result. And, yes, it is about hard work and having an approach that makes you study on the train on the way to work, in lines at the grocery store, and on Saturday nights while your friends and family are out having fun. It's about respecting your study plan and refusing to let study time scheduled for today be put off until tomorrow.

Everyone has heard of the university professor of a difficult math or science class who tells his students on the first day of class, "Look to your left and right. Say goodbye, because only one of you will be left at the end of this course. The rest will fail or quit." Instead, imagine a professor saying, "Look to your left, your right, and then seven other people. Out of the ten of you, one may still be here at the end. And really, I can't promise that." We must be a little crazy to sign up for such a course. Those of us who stick it out must be even crazier. However, this is also why CFA charterholders command professional and personal respect.

Just by signing up for the CFA Program, you've already earned some of that respect; I'll try to help you become that last person standing. You can pass these exams. All you need is a sensible, sometimes unique approach paired with sustained determination.

Now is the time to start the CFA Program. You can do this if you implement an appropriate study plan and choose to follow it with absolute resolve. You might feel unsure as you begin, but every CFA charterholder was once a candidate just like you. You are capable of becoming a CFA charterholder. With the right mix of tools and strategies, you can pass the CFA Program.

This book leads you on a direct path towards your CFA charter, and you can begin walking down that path today.

PART ONE

Answers to Big Questions

ANSWERS TO BIG QUESTIONS

You have important questions about the CFA Program and need insightful answers. You're looking for more than conventional advice; you crave powerful, actionable wisdom that can make a substantial difference in your exam results. You might be equally concerned about the questions you don't know to ask. Are there things you're missing—crucial discoveries you need to make before it's too late?

Part One answers your burning questions about the CFA Program and addresses others that you might not have thought to ask. You will gain essential, uncommon know-how for building a CFA-exam strategy that achieves passing scores on the first try. When you reach Part Two, you will be equipped with practical knowledge that will be vital to shaping your study regimen.

You're likely aware that few people pass the CFA exams, particularly on the first try. However, you may not know the systematic reasons *why* these candidates pass and others don't. It is not because they study hard. Most candidates study hard. It is not because they are splendidly smarter than other candidates. Instead, successful candidates discover the CFA Program's underlying factors and then follow a study regimen that maneuvers through the Program with savvy, determined effort. Most candidates are intellectually capable of passing the CFA exams; a limited number translate that capability into passing scores.

The biggest conclusion I hope you'll make from these chapters (and this entire book) is that few candidates pass the CFA exams, so you need an approach that few candidates take. There are secrets and strategies to succeeding in the CFA Program that many candidates never discover. You want to know these insights now to take a direct path to the CFA charter. Part One is the first stage to uncovering these insights to help you pass the exams and, as a CFA charterholder, move on with your career.

CHAPTER 1

CFA Program Overview

Before diving into the juicy details of how to attack the CFA Program, let's cover the basics. You should understand the CFA Program's scope and structure before proceeding. After this chapter, the rest of the book assumes that you know the fundamentals.

As you'll see from the "basic" factors, the CFA Program isn't particularly basic. Sometimes the CFA Program can seem mysterious and complicated. Over the next few pages, I'll simplify it. Even if you're already familiar with the Program's fundamentals, a refresher never hurts (and I'll move through this quickly).

Five Main Features of the CFA Program

In short, the CFA Program is a graduate-level, self-study course that teaches investment management concepts. Candidates in the Program hope to pass three CFA exams and become a CFA charterholder, which is a highly respected credential in the financial industry.

If you haven't done so already, I suggest pausing to take some time to poke around the CFA Institute website at www.cfainstitute.org. The website is not especially easy to navigate but ultimately explains the CFA Program from the viewpoint of the organization that creates the tests and awards the CFA charter. Thus, the CFA Institute's website is worth reading.

The CFA Program sports five main features. While there is more to it than these five points, they are the base on which you'll build a winning strategy. The Program:

1. Consists of three exams that must be passed, in order, over a minimum of two years
2. Develops a unique theme for each of the three tests
3. Covers ten areas of finance related to investing
4. Provides textbooks (known as curriculum books) that contain everything candidates are required to learn
5. Establishes rules on how to refer to your participation in the CFA Program

The following pages walk through these five points with an eye towards what you need to know to set yourself up for success. If this is your first time exploring the CFA Program, this chapter might feel like I am pouring a giant bucket of CFA information over your head. Don't worry; soon you'll be so comfortable with the Program that you'll be coaching other candidates on it. Every person who now holds a CFA charter was at some time new to the Program. Take your time and, remember, you're beginning a life-altering quest! Be proud of yourself and stay enthusiastic.

1) Three Exams over Two Years or More

The CFA Program spans across three tests that must be completed in order: Level I, Level II, and Level III. (The CFA Institute uses roman numerals to designate between the Levels which is why I do so throughout this book as well.) For all Levels, the exams are six hours long. The Level I and II tests are wholly made up of multiple-choice questions. For Level III, half of the exam consists of multiple-choice questions, while the other half presents essay questions.

The Levels won't go by quickly. Each test necessitates roughly six months of study time to pass. In total, candidates study almost every day for at least 18 months to pass the three exams.

Stretching the timeline out further, the CFA Institute only offers each exam once or twice per year. These tests differ from many other professional examinations which may be taken on practically any day you choose.

Rather, the Level I exam is offered twice per year in June and December, while Levels II and III are only offered once in June. Once per year! Half your time in the CFA Program is spent studying, while the other half is spent waiting until it's time to gear up for the next Level.

Candidates must complete the Levels in succession—no skipping ahead or taking more than one Level at a time. Consequently, there's no way to speed the Program up; the CFA Institute offers the exams on these dates, and that's that.

Therefore, because of the infrequent testing opportunities, the CFA Program requires at least a two-year commitment from the day you begin studying for the Level I exam to the date of your Level III exam. Most candidates take longer. Completing the Program in two years is only possible if you take the Level I test in December, the Level II test the following June, and the Level III test the next June—and pass each on your first try. Personally, I took two-and-a-half years because I sat for the Level I exam in June instead of December (which I recommend for you also in Chapter 8, "A Study Plan from Start to Finish"). Whatever your track, commitment is a big part of this experience.

Failing a Level is costly. Failing Level I burns six months while you wait to repeat the test, while failing Level II or III consumes another twelve months. Because this is such an incredibly important point that I cannot emphasize enough, let me reiterate: failing Level II or III will cost you an *entire year*! Repeating just one test can tack on a year to your CFA Program stint, turning this two-year program into a three-year one. Failing again adds on another year; we're now at four, the length of an undergraduate degree. One more, and a PhD in finance would have taken the same amount of time. This is the most dangerous aspect of the CFA Program. This is why I want to help you to avoid repeating Levels. It costs time and money.

If you weren't previously thinking about this as a graduate-level, challenging course, I hope that you are now. Most graduate degrees are earned in less time than CFA charters. As your friends finish their Certificates of Public Accountancy (CPAs), Master of Business (MBA) degrees, and the like, you keep chugging along.

For the pleasure of taking these tests, you'll have to cough up some cash. Like any other professional certification, the CFA Program charges test fees for every CFA exam you take. Many employers will help with these test fees; check with yours before beginning the CFA Program. Keep in mind that if a candidate fails a Level and tries again, he or she must pay the test fee again.

At the time of this writing, the CFA Institute requires a $440 "first time enrollment fee" to register for the Level I test, which is marketing speak for "give us your money for no reason."[3] On top of that fee, exam registration for each Level costs $620 if you meet a very early deadline, $800 if you register with most everyone else, or $1,170 if you procrastinate. Therefore, Level I costs between $1,060 and $1,610. Thankfully, you don't have to pay the enrollment fee in Levels II and III. When all said and done, the Program will cost a few thousand dollars in fees.

On the extremely bright side, a master's degree often costs a lot more. Every certification has its price, and in comparison the CFA charter might have the best return on investment that exists in the business world.

However, when you attain the CFA designation, for the rest of your career the CFA Institute charges approximately $300 per year for the privilege of using the certification you've earned. This brings the total cost of the CFA designation to roughly $15,000 over a typical career assuming you earn the CFA charter before your 30th birthday. A nuisance, but still less than the master's degree. Also, positively, you don't have to pay this money up front. Congratulations! You just learned the CFA Program's first lesson in the time value of money.

The CFA Program is a journey that requires patience, resolve, time, and money. Give it apt forethought and reflection before jumping in.

2) A Unique Theme for Each Test

The Program proceeds in an orderly fashion with each Level reflecting a unique theme: Foundation, Application, and Mastery. Each Level achieves a heightened stage of proficiency beyond the previous one.

Level I builds a solid foundation in every topic. It is massive. The subject matter isn't particularly difficult, but the sheer volume defeats many candidates. If you have an undergraduate degree in finance, Level I may be easier for you than others. Though, I had an undergraduate degree specializing in finance and Level I was a challenge because of its size. You should expect a big undertaking irrespective of your background.

Next, Level II focuses on application of theories, concepts, and equations in real life situations. You might have financial knowledge, but Level II determines if you can apply it. Every question contains some trick or nuance, which makes for an extremely challenging exam. Candidates typically name Level II as the most difficult, as it was for me. Level II tests more than your understanding of the curriculum; it tests your willpower.

Finally, Level III makes sure that you've mastered the CFA Program's subject matter. You'll demonstrate that you can bring the testing topics together, think holistically, and deliver solutions to your clients with exceptional expertise. Candidates often identify Level III as the most enjoyable because it best aligns with what we want to do in our jobs on a day-to-day basis. That doesn't mean it's easy. Level III presents some unique challenges which, like the other two Levels, can be overcome with suitable strategies that I'll outline in later chapters.

Foundation, application, and mastery. These themes make for a structured program that has purpose every step of the way. With such different objectives at each stage, the CFA Program won't be monotonous.

3) Topics Included on the CFA Tests

If nothing else, the CFA Program is thorough. You'll study almost every financial topic under the sun.

According to the CFA Institute, these are the ten subjects that are covered on the CFA tests:[4]

1. Ethical and Professional Standards
2. Quantitative Methods
3. Economics
4. Financial Reporting and Analysis
5. Corporate Finance
6. Alternative Investments
7. Equity Investments
8. Fixed Income
9. Derivatives
10. Portfolio Management and Wealth Planning

It's as if the CFA Institute held a contest asking people to name every finance-related topic they could think of and this was the winning entry. The exams span a wide range of financial topics that barely stop short of adjacent fields such as accounting, financial planning, etc. Actually, you'll get a healthy dose of those topics as well since they are sprinkled throughout the ten testable areas. Basically, these exams touch every branch of finance, which means you're about to have empathy for your general care doctor— it's a tall order to be a generalist and have a working understanding of seemingly everything.

4) The Infamous Curriculum Books

You may be wondering how you'll learn about the ten exam areas. Basically, the CFA Program is a series of college courses without a professor, so textbooks rule your days.

When you sign up for a CFA test, the CFA Institute sends you six textbooks containing that Level's "Candidate Body of Knowledge," or CBOK. Over several months, you'll learn everything in the CBOK books, which contain what you need to know to answer every test question. Candidates refer to them as the curriculum books.

You'll finish the CFA Program with about 18 curriculum books. Your bookshelf is going to look very impressive! Every Level's registration comes with six books packed with new material. When it is all said and done, you will have, in effect, memorized all eighteen textbooks. This is doable because you will learn them in pieces and over time.

When you register for a Level and pay your test fees, you're also paying for that Level's curriculum books. Hopefully, this makes the test fees easier to swallow—the money buys useful reference materials. You can opt to study the curriculum books in e-book format, however, I strongly caution against this option. Practice questions, examples, and other facets of the curriculum books are best seen in physical form. The exams are given with pencil and paper, so use printed study materials whenever possible.

The answer to every test question can be found in your curriculum books, which are compiled by the CFA Institute. Therefore, the books are similar to university textbooks in that they are your study material. However, unlike university textbooks, you must learn every crumb of information. Nothing may be skimmed, skipped, or ignored.

To hone your focus, the books' readings come with Learning Outcome Statements (LOSs). Learning Outcome Statements describe exactly what skills and abilities the CFA Institute believes you should have acquired from your studying efforts. Every question on test day can be linked to a Learning Outcome Statement. The CFA Institute's website contains many examples of LOSs that I would have liked to quote here. However, it appears that the CFA Institute requires special permission and a licensing fee.[5] To keep this book's price down, I've made up similarly worded examples related to the sport of soccer:

- Calculate the probability of a goal assist from midfield.
- Determine the optimal formation for offensive players given the field's weather conditions.
- Explain the off-sides penalty and demonstrate its application.
- Construct a defense strategy that minimizes the risk of goals scored by the opposing team.

Notice the command words in these soccer LOSs: "determine," "calculate," "explain," "demonstrate," and "construct." As you study, pay special attention to the command words in each LOS; if the LOS only requires that you explain a concept, don't waste your time learning how to demonstrate it. It is the CFA Institute's policy to only expect the proficiency requested by each Learning Outlook Statement and no more.[6]

By providing LOSs, the CFA Institute essentially gives you a hint into what the test questions will assess. Accordingly, keep these LOSs in mind as you study. Confirm that you have achieved each learning outcome.

For each Level, to help us navigate the LOSs, the CFA Institute divides them into 18 study sessions. Each study session is basically a collection of a few informational readings and practice problems related to one topic, all of which you'll need to learn. For instance, the Derivatives study session might contain three academic papers and a few dozen practice problems. You'll study all of this as a cohesive unit. Each curriculum book contains a few of these study sessions, which you'll learn during your test preparation. (Many third-party companies offer test prep systems that complement the curriculum books; I'll cover them in detail in

Part Two, "Study Regimen." I also provide a list of test preparation resources and descriptions of each in the back of the book.)

As I mentioned earlier, the books cover 10 testing subjects but have 18 study sessions. Hence, larger topics are spread across two study sessions. For example, in Level I, the smaller Alternative Investments topic only needs one study session, while the larger Financial Reporting and Analysis topic might extend across two sessions.

Every study session is clearly mapped to one of the 10 core testing topics. Because my recommended study plan (and generally everyone else's study plan) revolves around the 18 study sessions rather than the 10 overarching topics, I'll normally refer to the 18 study sessions when helping you plan your study regimen.

In the end, we have six books in each Level, which contain 18 study sessions, which contain numerous readings, which contain LOSs. The CFA Program centers on these books.

5) Referring to Yourself as a CFA Candidate

Perhaps you're enthused by the idea of curriculum books and Learning Outcome Statements (LOSs) and want to move forward with registering for the CFA Level I test. If you've completed your registration, you may call yourself a "Level I CFA candidate" or simply a "CFA candidate." These are the proper terms to display on résumés, business cards, social media websites, etc. However, you may not put these terms after your name, as in "John Doe, CFA Candidate." Only CFA charterholders may use the CFA letters after their names.

Further, calling yourself a "Level I CFA" is always a no-no. You are a Level I CFA *candidate*. When you pass the Level I exam and register for Level II, you are a Level II CFA *candidate*. Until you earn the CFA charter, the word "candidate" must always accompany any description of your participation in the Program. You can't suggest that you achieved a partial designation by calling yourself a "Level II CFA" or the like.

These are not my rules. The CFA Institute's *Code of Ethics and Standards of Professional Conduct (Code and Standards)* governs your participation in the Program, including edicts on exactly how you may refer to yourself as a CFA candidate. You must agree to abide by the *Code and Standards* when you register for the tests. Ignore the rules and you may be kicked out of the Program or denied a CFA charter. More likely, finance professionals who are familiar with the Program will recognize that you're purposefully breaking the rules, which doesn't make you look too good.

There's an important distinction between people planning to take a CFA exam and candidates actually registered for one. Perhaps you want to read a few more chapters of this book before you're ready to take the plunge and register for the Level I test. Until you do, the ethics rules state that you're not a CFA candidate and can't use that moniker. Planning to sign up for the CFA Program does not establish you as a CFA candidate. To call yourself a CFA candidate, you must be either registered to sit for a CFA exam or awaiting the results from an exam that you just took.

Let's pretend you recently sat for the Level I exam and are awaiting your scores, which are due in two months. You may call yourself a CFA candidate during this time while you patiently (or maybe not so patiently) wait for the results. Fast forward several weeks and pretend that you just received a passing score on that Level I exam. Suddenly, you're no longer a CFA candidate until you register for the Level II test. You might have every intention to take the Level II exam, but you must register for it to be considered a CFA candidate.

You may be saying to yourself, "this all seems a bit ridiculous." These rules may seem heavy handed, but they are trying to discern between professionals who are actually in the CFA Program and those who claim to be but are not. I fully support these rules because there are professionals who quit the Program after Level I or II but continue describing themselves as CFA candidates forever. This purposefully misleads their clients and employers. These people have no intention of taking another CFA test in the near future, but they continue calling themselves CFA candidates to give the impression that they're pursuing higher education. Unethical behavior like this reflects badly on our industry. And, it's unfair to true candidates.

The ethics criterion might seem insignificant at first but, when they are disregarded, it detracts from the value of the designation you're working hard to get. You can help protect the charter's integrity by following the rules and only calling yourself a CFA candidate when it is appropriate to do so. CFA charterholders appreciate and respect candidates who follow the ethics standards, as you will, too.

Piecing Together the Big Picture

This is a lot to take in, and I understand if you're overwhelmed; I've essentially condensed a multi-year experience into a few pages. To summarize, think of the CFA Program as a series of structured, controlled events. You will attempt Level I, you will wait a couple of months to find out if you passed, and then, assuming you are successful, you will proceed to Level II the next year. Assuming you're successful again, Level III follows. The tests cover 10 financial subjects that are related to managing investments. The CFA Institute will send you approximately six books at each Level containing all the information that you need to know. The CFA Institute's Learning Outcome Statements (LOSs) guide your studying effort. You must wait until you are registered for a CFA test to call yourself a CFA candidate. See, not so complicated after all.

Make sure you've taken a few minutes to explore the CFA Program area of the CFA Institute's website at http://www.cfainstitute.org/programs/cfaprogram. Again, you'll find information on the goals, structure, and requirements of the CFA Program directly from the organization that will be testing you: the CFA Institute. You'll also find statistics on passing rates, number of registrations in recent years, and other interesting tidbits of information.

Going forward, I'll assume that you understand the general aspects of the CFA Program and won't irk you with recitation. If you become confused, consider reviewing this chapter, revisiting the CFA Institute website, or performing a good old internet search. Also, please feel free to email questions or musings to me at rachel@rachel-bryant.com.

The next few chapters help gain resolution to some of the most interesting and burning disputes in the CFA Program. Your choices regarding the following issues are extremely influential in determining whether or not you will pass the CFA exams.

Key Takeaways: CFA Program Overview

- The CFA Program consists of three exams which must be completed in order: Level I, Level II, and Level III.

- Level I builds a foundation, Level II focuses on application of concepts, and Level III masters the practice of investment finance.

- The Level I test is given twice per year (June and December), while the Level II and Level III tests are only given once per year (June).

- The CFA exams cover ten topics:
  1. Ethical and Professional Standards
  2. Quantitative Methods
  3. Economics
  4. Financial Reporting and Analysis
  5. Corporate Finance
  6. Alternative Investments
  7. Equity Investments
  8. Fixed Income
  9. Derivatives
  10. Portfolio Management and Wealth Planning

- The test registration fees also pay for your Level's curriculum books, which contain all the information that will be tested on the exam.

- Learning Outcome Statements (LOSs) direct candidates to the most important skills and abilities that will be tested. Pay special attention to each LOSs' command words; you are only expected to attain the proficiency indicated by these guidelines.

- The curriculum books contain 18 study sessions that address the 10 testing topics and organize the LOSs.

- The CFA Institute's *Code of Ethics and Standards of Professional Conduct (Code and Standards)* governs how candidates should refer to participation in the CFA Program.

- A person may adopt the label of CFA candidate if, and only if, he or she is registered to sit for a CFA test or is awaiting test results.

- The terms "CFA candidate" or "Level I CFA candidate" are appropriate terms for referencing your candidacy, not "Level I CFA."

- The CFA Program can seem complicated at first, but soon these main tenets will become second nature. Keep up your positive, can-do attitude—you'll get the hang of it!

CHAPTER 2

Does Industry Experience Matter?

In the introduction to Part One, I promised you would learn the underlying reasons why some candidates pass the CFA exams and others do not. You might be wondering if industry experience is one of these factors. If you have industry experience, you probably hope it matters a lot. If you have none, you're hoping industry experience doesn't matter so much. The reality is that industry experience is less important than how you adapt to the CFA Program given your situation.

The Benefits and Limits of Industry Experience

There are some positives to having industry experience in the CFA Program, but they aren't significant game changers. Having work experience is only vaguely helpful because a typical professional's job is specific, and these exams are broad. Targeted knowledge may help a little but it won't make a big difference on tests that include almost every financial topic that exists.

The corporate world is all about specialization, particularly in the first two decades of your career. As a result, even those of us with numerous years in the industry tend to have narrow experience. Finance professionals rarely have jobs that engage more than two or three areas of the CFA curriculum. For this reason, a person's industry experience might be beneficial, but only on a small fraction of the test.

For example, I work in risk management within the banking sector, and I would probably score well in the few areas directly related to this experience. On the other hand, in my daily work, I do not draw supply-demand charts (like you will in the Economics study section), calculate net present value of acquisitions (Corporate Finance), trade stripped bonds (Fixed Income), implement option strategies (Equity Investments), create retiree portfolio allocation plans (Wealth Management), or apply dozens of other skills you'll learn in the CFA Program. I lean on the general lessons learned from almost every topic in the CFA Program, but I could only test well in the few areas that I deal with on a regular basis. If I were starting out in the CFA Program today, with most topics, I would have the same familiarity as candidates straight out of college.

This is typical. Those with industry experience have lots of knowledge about specific subjects but may have little knowledge of others. So, industry experience has some value, but it doesn't drastically alter the experienced person's prospects.

That is not to say that industry experience has no significance. Let's step outside of finance for a moment and say you want to become an airplane pilot. Imagine you've never seen an airplane in real life. You are aware that planes exist and you read about them a lot. But to this point in time, you've never visited an airport or ridden in a plane as a passenger. You have no concrete experience with airplanes. Now we're going to introduce you to a jetliner, hand you a written manual, and have you flying in a few weeks.

Not going to happen, right? This airplane thing is totally new. You need time to digest not just the flying instructions but the airplane itself. With time and adequate education materials, you'll figure it out. But it's going to be a steeper hill than for the person who lives next to an airfield.

Flying a plane with no pre-understanding of how planes work is similar to passing the CFA exams with no pre-understanding of capital markets. It's doable. Just doable at a slower pace.

The benefit of having industry experience (perhaps five years or more) is a comfort level with the industry vocabulary, concepts, and jargon that are packed into the CFA curriculum. Learning how to calculate the pricing on a forward-rate agreement (FRA) is a lot easier when your first thought isn't, "What's an FRA?" Even if you have a passion for finance and religiously follow all of the major market indicators, the CFA Program is tougher without the foundation of financial experience.

Don't let lack of experience keep you from trying. The Program is passable without any industry experience. You simply need to study a bit extra to overpower your experience deficit.

I started the Program with two years of experience but, truthfully, I felt like I had none. Everything was still so new that it seemed like I had just graduated. I knew I was inexperienced and would need to do something to make up for it. So I accepted the fact that my lack of experience meant extra hours of studying in each Level. Honestly, when you're already altering your life to make room for hundreds of hours of study time, adding a bit more isn't particularly noticeable. If you maintain a strong work ethic and study in a methodical way, you won't be held back by a shortage of hands-on experience.

If you are newly entering the financial industry, I recommend starting the CFA Program as soon as you're ready. There's little to gain by waiting, and a lot to gain by finishing it while you're young. You'll have more years to enjoy the fruits of your labor.

On test day, industry experience means very little as long as those who lack industry experience do what it takes to place themselves on an even footing with the finance veterans. Besides, a person can have a job title and description that the CFA Institute would heartily approve while actually spending his or days surfing the internet. Don't let "industry experience" intimidate you.

In fact, having industry experience can be a burden. If you have lots of experience, you're facing a different obstacle. Instead of an experience deficit, you likely have a time deficit.

Veterans don't have tons of time to study the information. Having time makes all the difference. Seasoned professionals tend to have a spouse, perhaps a couple of kids, and a house to maintain. After factoring in work hours, time with the family, and general life upkeep, there's little time left. How will fifteen hours of study time be found every week? Maybe for a month or two, you can find the time for a consistent study schedule. Studying for six months straight at least three times will be a considerable challenge. Some weeks your life just won't have room for studying, which is a serious disadvantage.

The younger professionals tend to have fewer commitments outside of work and therefore can devote more time to studying. Who do you think will pass: the skilled professional who only had time to look at each equation once, or the 22-year-old amateur who reviewed each equation three times and performed examples of each? I'm putting my money on the amateur because, out of hundreds of equations, I bet the veteran doesn't regularly work with more than 30. To learn the rest, the industry veteran needs good old-fashioned study time.

Besides having the time, fresh college graduates are comfortable with exams and textbooks as a normal part of life. They may be novices in finance, but they're experts in studying. In comparison, beginning a study regimen when you haven't taken a test in 15 years can be a harsh adjustment.

If you have oodles of experience, don't be overconfident. Lots of 20-somethings will receive charters this year while plenty of industry mavens will fail. There's a lot to learn in the CFA Program for professionals of all backgrounds and experience levels. Because the test covers so many subjects, at least 50 percent of the topics are likely to be unfamiliar to you. Overestimating the value of your experience can be a fatal mistake.

However, your prior knowledge can help you absorb the curriculum faster and make it stick. The shift from newcomer to practitioner seems to occur around five years of experience. Having at least five years in the industry often means having an easier time with the curriculum. With ten years or more, your expertise can mean sailing through a whole topic now and then. As long as you are careful to review everything (even if swiftly for some subjects), you will be well-positioned to compete with the rookies who studied their hearts out.

Work Experience Requirements

There is one reason why all candidates want and need industry experience: at least four years are required to qualify for the CFA charter. The four years (or 48 months) don't have to be consecutive nor conform to the annual calendar; the total is what matters.[7] The

CFA Institute requires this minimum level of industry experience to make sure that the CFA charter is awarded to industry professionals—not individuals hoping to get into the industry. This communicates that CFA charterholders have real-world experience to give weight to their credentials.

There are no industry experience requirements to participate in the CFA *Program*—the four year requirement only applies to granting of the CFA charter. You can start the CFA Program with no experience at all, as long as you are in your final year of a bachelor's degree. This means, though, that you may pass all the tests before you're eligible for the charter. Then you'll have to wait

until the 48 months come and go before applying for the charter. Be aware that passing the exams isn't the only to-do item on your list; you need experience, too.

Not every "financial" job counts as CFA Institute-approved experience. For example, doing general ledger reconciliations all day isn't going to meet the criteria. At least half of your working hours must be spent doing CFA Institute-approved activities that are related to making investment decisions. Examples of such activities include equities research, fixed income analysis,

management consulting, implementing trading strategies, portfolio management, risk management, quantitative analysis, economic research, auditing financial statements, forming actuarial projections, etc. Check the CFA Institute website for the current guidelines.

Check the website today, not after you've passed the three CFA exams. Verify how your previous experience and that expected over the next few years stack up to the CFA Institute's policy. You don't want to find out later that the CFA Institute won't accept your experience.

If you don't have an approved job, consider outlining a five-year plan before undertaking the CFA Program. Having passed one or all of the CFA tests sometimes helps candidates get their feet in the doors of finance companies or departments, but you won't qualify for the CFA charter until you've worked in the industry for a total of 48 months.

Whether you have lots of experience or barely make the four-year requirement, you'll have to prove your experience before the CFA Institute will award the charter. You'll need to explain exactly how your day-to-day responsibilities have a bearing on the investment-decision making process. After you pass all the CFA tests, you'll submit a description of your job responsibilities for the CFA Institute's consideration. Don't force a "no." Give adequate detail so the Institute can easily see how your work relates to investing.

Additionally, the Institute requires three personal recommendations to earn the charter, unless one is from a regular member of your local society. In that case, you only need two references.

Though the process of getting your work experience approved sounds like awaiting judgment day, in reality, it's not so bad. The qualification criteria are broadcast on the CFA Institute's website; as long as you meet the criteria, you'll get the charter.

You'll be busy in the CFA Program, but try to manage your career while also managing your study regimen. If the CFA charter is on your radar, you'll need industry experience eventually. You might not need it to pass the tests, but you will need work experience to earn your charter.

Industry Experience Does Not Determine Who Succeeds

In this program, industry experience isn't all it's cracked up to be. Those with industry experience often have less opportunity to study, while those without experience have more. By test day, everyone is pretty even. This is why industry experience is not a deciding factor in who succeeds in the CFA Program; your study regimen is. If you don't have much experience, simply study longer and harder.

If you do have ample experience, know that fresh college graduates can usually study harder than you because they don't have your other responsibilities. Know what you're signing up for and give it all that you can.

Both veterans and new hires will encounter unique challenges in the CFA Program. Whatever your situation, address it through your study routine.

Key Takeaways: Does Industry Experience Matter?

- You can be successful in the CFA Program, regardless if you lack industry experience. Simply schedule extra time in your study regimen to familiarize yourself with new concepts.

- If you have lots of industry experience, this can be an asset as long as you make time to study. Cover every topic to be sure that your practical knowledge matches the curriculum teachings. Also be alert to the breadth of the CFA exams; in contrast, your experience might be targeted.

- Four years (or 48 months) of investment-related, financial-industry experience are required before the CFA Institute will grant the CFA charter. Even if you pass the tests, you won't qualify until you've completed four years of work experience.

- The CFA Institute publishes its current work-experience guidelines on its website. Don't assume that your experience meets the expectations; check into this now, not after you've passed the exams.

CHAPTER 3

The First Secret to Passing CFA Exams: Strategize for the English Language

This fundamental truth of the CFA Program has an outsized influence on why some candidates succeed and others don't: the CFA exams are only offered in the English language. This presents an advantage for some candidates and a disadvantage for others. Depending on your fluency with English, you can tailor your study regimen to exploit this potential advantage or overcome this potential obstacle.

The CFA Program operates on a global scale with participants in almost every country on the planet, but the CFA Program centers around one language. It doesn't matter where you physically sit for the CFA exams; they are presented in English.

This one fact will affect your experience as a CFA Candidate from start to finish.

Many candidates enter the CFA Program not realizing how the single language affects them, for good or bad. The camp you fall into—native English speaker or not—has implications for your study regimen and your test results. Candidates who lack a native speaker's command of the English language are at a distinct disadvantage on the CFA exams versus those who speak English as their first language. Strategizing around this fact is a secret to passing the CFA exams for both groups, though in different ways.

The CFA Institute plainly states that the CFA exams are only given in English; you must confirm that you understand this before you can complete the registration process to sign up for an exam. What candidates may not know is that getting through all three Levels is much tougher if you don't read and write English quickly.

Candidates from all corners of the globe succeed in the CFA Program, so the secret isn't to magically make English your native tongue. Instead, the secret is knowing your odds of success before you begin studying so that you can adjust those odds through your study plan.

Both native English speakers and non-native speakers can and do pass, but you should tailor your approach to your circumstances. Overpower a disadvantage with more effort or, on the other hand, use an advantage to help alleviate anxiety.

A Truly Worldwide Designation

(A quick note to my neighbors in North and South America: For brevity's sake throughout this chapter, I occasionally use the term "Americans" to refer to people from the United States of America, including myself. I recognize that you are Americans in a different context. Thanks for understanding why United States of America citizens—see how long that is!—embrace and cherish the American moniker.)

The organization that runs the CFA Program, the CFA Institute, is based in the United States. This helps explain why a program spanning the globe adheres to the United States' predominantly spoken language. However, according to the CFA Institute's website, the Asia–Pacific region was the largest source of CFA-test takers in 2013 accounting for 44 percent of the total.[8] Nearly half! Another 21 percent were from Europe, the Middle East, and Africa. The Americas, which include numerous Spanish- and French-speaking countries, rounded out the remaining 35 percent of candidates. Many candidates hail from regions that overwhelmingly speak languages other than English as their first. As you can see, this is a worldwide designation, not an exclusively American one.

A total of 168 countries were represented at the June 2013 exams, which is remarkable reach for a designation bestowed on less than 200,000 people since its founding. On test day, professionals from countless cultures are sitting down for the same exams. This is pretty special. Candidates worldwide are collectively saying "yes" to better personal prospects and a better industry. You might feel a sense of camaraderie knowing that candidates everywhere are as nervous as you. Regardless of our diverse cultures, we're all reaching for the same goal and we're all about to have the same experience. Well, almost.

As a native English speaker and an American, I had an inherent advantage over many other candidates on test day. Tens of thousands of candidates take these tests in a language that is not their native one. You may have learned English at an early age. But still, it will always be a second (or third or fourth) language. This issue receives little commentary from candidates, charterholders, or the media, which is a mystery to me. Command of the English language is imperative to succeed.

The CFA Program's study materials are only available in English, as well. The curriculum books, third-party review systems, practice tests, and other tools match the exams' language.

Like most Americans, I know only the one language I use every day. I've always been impressed with the multi-lingual abilities of people in most other parts of the world. My ancestors are from Italy, so I tried learning Italian a few years ago. I couldn't believe how hard it was to learn a new language! I never got past the most basic vocabulary. And Italian and English share a common alphabet; I can't imagine being fluent in a radically dissimilar language. Really, I can't imagine being fluent in another language at all. If you are, count me as amazed.

Unfortunately, my respect likely does not provide much comfort on exams that are only written in one language. The CFA Institute explains that the tests are only given in English "in order to ensure global consistency, both in administering the exam questions and in grading candidate responses."[9] I ponder as to why bilingual CFA charterholders couldn't reliably translate the exams into other languages, since books, newspapers, and other exams are reliably translated every day. Giving the tests in every language would be impossibly cumbersome but, perhaps, the CFA Institute could offer the exams in four or five of the most common languages to ensure that the CFA charter continues to be recognized and respected throughout the world as an elite designation for years to come.

In fairness to the CFA Institute, there is a saying that English is the international language of finance. The CFA Program's approach marries with the industry's use of English. Positively, participating in the CFA Program is an opportunity to both learn finance and gain skills in the industry's common language. This accomplishes two objectives with one activity. In America, we would say this is hitting two birds with one stone. (To be clear, Americans do not throw things at birds. In fact, we're more likely to set out expensive birdseed and shoo predators away to make sure the bird lives longer than we do.)

Revealing that the single language may be affecting results, the geographic dispersion of charterholders does not reflect the geographic dispersion of candidates. Charters are more often awarded to candidates in English-speaking countries, even though they represent a small portion of all candidates.

Of all charters awarded in 2013, only 25 percent went to the Asia–Pacific region, though it fielded 44 percent of CFA candidates.[10] There are smart, capable candidates in every country, so this suggests there may be a language hurdle. In contrast, the Americas (containing the United States) received 48 percent of all charters in 2013, though it only fielded 35 percent of candidates. Europe, the Middle East, and Africa earned 26 percent of new charters while yielding 21 percent of candidates. Most tellingly, almost half of all charters earned globally in 2013 went to two countries that just happen to speak English as their first language: the United States and the United Kingdom. It seems that candidates in non-English speaking countries contend with obstacles that other candidates don't have to, and this shows up in test results.

The Advantages Bestowed on English Speakers

If you're in the native minority, you're almost assured of making it through Level I if you put in a reasonable number of study hours (discussed in Chapter 7, "The 300-Hour Trap"). Thousands of people in Level I are either unprepared or hesitating over the English language, or both. They are your competition. While they worry about deciphering a given question, you only have to worry about answering it. You will also absorb the curriculum more easily than non-native speakers.

You have the luxury of following the study regimen I outline in Part B of this book, rather than adding to it. You still need to study very hard but your strong preparation and English-speaking advantage will together increase your odds of success.

If you're from the United States, the advantage is even larger. It might be taboo to say, but the CFA Institute is an American institution and these tests reflect that fact. American securities laws, jargon, and methods are highlighted. If you are an American, only your lack of preparation will hold you back in Level I.

An advantage will persist in Level II, though it will narrow somewhat. Non-native candidates who move forward to Level II have demonstrated that they can overcome language barriers, whether it be with hard work or mastery of the English language, or both. Yet, native speakers still enjoy an advantage in Level II due to the time crunch on this test that probably didn't exist at Level I. Some non-native speaking candidates will be caught off guard.

The advantage will persist through Level III, as well, particularly on the essay portion of the test. Online forums are littered with Level III candidates contemplating if they should quit the Program because they can't execute on the essay questions. However, by this point, every candidate has demonstrated financial expertise. Some might be battling forces beyond the curriculum, but many of these candidates will work harder than you, thus overcoming their language disadvantage.

By Level III, everyone is hungry for a passing exam score. Starving, actually. Level III candidates are tired of the years of studying and want their lives back. Therefore, you should pretend that the English-speaking advantage doesn't exist in Level III as very few people let it defeat them in the long run.

Overall, a study regimen that is moderately enhanced compared to the typical candidate should propel the native speaker into the likely passing category. Many people won't adequately prepare, regardless of what language they speak. You will be positioned to compete with these ill-prepared candidates and execute on your English skills.

Nevertheless, passing numbers are limited. I would view my English-speaking advantage as a reason to sleep better at night, not a reason to study equal to or less than average.

I Learned English as a Second Language—Can I Pass?

Perhaps you must take the CFA tests in a language other than your native one. I feel for you. The playing field is essentially unfair. However, the CFA Institute does not make you sign up for the CFA Program; you knowingly choose to participate. There's nothing you can do about the fairness of this issue. Instead, I'll lay out a plan to conquer it.

Passing is possible. Thousands of non-native English speakers pass these tests every year. Granted, thousands more fail. I want to help you avoid that fate.

Simply put, you'll have to work harder if you lack fluency in the English language. Your challenge is not in learning the curriculum. You can always research any foreign terms on the internet, and study notes from a third-party vendor can clarify confusing points. Instead, finishing the tests within the allotted time may be your main difficulty. There's not much time on these exams for hesitation. Even native speakers are still scribbling answers as time is called on the Level II and III tests.

When the proctor announced the end of my Level II test, I looked around at my fellow Americans and noticed that no one had left early. We all worked until the last second. Some didn't finish, even though they knew the language and the jargon.

And let us not forget the essay portion of Level III. There are candidates who have languished for years in Level III because they are not only battling the tests but also the language. These candidates are having trouble completing the essays in the time allotted.

As a non-native speaker, plan to know the curriculum more deeply than your English-speaking counterparts. This should make up for these time concerns. If you know the curriculum better than native speakers, you can still hesitate over an English word here and there and still pass.

Practice tests will be a particularly important study activity for you; consider completing seven or more practice tests, rather than the four I usually recommend (see Chapter 11, "Transforming Knowledge into Test Performance"). Aim to finish each practice test in five hours instead of the test day allotment of six. All candidates are slower on test day, so this discipline can rescue you when it matters. Really push yourself.

I also recommend starting your study regimen a bit early. In Chapter 8, "A Study Plan from Start to Finish," I discuss my opinion on when candidates should start studying for the CFA tests. You may have to start earlier than my recommended timeframe by at least one month, since you need time to delve deeper into the curriculum and complete extra practice tests.

Unfortunately, I can't tell you exactly how much additional time and effort you should plan to expend in your quest for the CFA charter since I don't know what languages you speak, how long you've been speaking English, or your comfort with the language. I admit that it's also hard for me to imagine how difficult it must be to approach these tests in a language other than the one I'm most comfortable with. I have nothing but the utmost respect for you. You're entering a program that is already difficult enough and, essentially, signing up for extra work.

Nonetheless, if you stick to a rigorous study schedule and wholeheartedly commit to the Program, the language issue usually won't hold you back. Numerous people have succeeded before you, and you can, too.

Though, I will be honest with you. There are no promises in the CFA Program. Many, actually *most*, candidates never receive a charter (see Chapter 6, "A Quiet, Important Statistic"). It takes bravery—or foolishness—to sign up for this program in the face of these realities. Whether you are brave or foolish largely depends on your preparation.

If earning the CFA charter is your goal, be willing to work harder than your native English-speaking counterparts. Prepare at the necessary intensity to overcome any disadvantage.

The Language You Speak Is Not a Verdict

The purpose of this discussion is not to scare you into quitting, or, inversely, thrill you into premature victory dances. I know from experience that uncertainty is a constant presence during the CFA Program for all candidates. I hope that knowing this secret about the CFA Program reduces a small part of the uncertainty.

Either way, the language you speak won't determine your performance; only your response to it will.

Thankfully, from here on out, the factors that can impact your CFA Program experience are fully within your control. Next, the second secret to passing CFA Levels can boost your performance no matter your native language.

Key Takeaways: The First Secret to Passing CFA Exams

- Candidates across the globe participate in the CFA Program. In 2013, 44 percent of candidates were from the Asia–Pacific region, 35 percent were from the Americas, and 21 percent were from Europe, the Middle East, and Africa. A total of 168 countries were represented in the June 2013 exams.

- The tests are only given in English regardless of the country's native language. Therefore, native English speakers—particularly those from the United States—have an advantage on the CFA tests.

- The disadvantage of speaking English as a second language can be overcome with additional effort and a smart study routine. Consider adding study hours, taking additional practice tests, and completing practice tests in five hours instead of six.

- Native speakers can follow the study regimen outlined in this book and pass. Let your command of the English language help you sleep at night.

CHAPTER 4

The Second Secret to Passing CFA Exams: Know Retiring Topics

In hindsight, charterholders often realize things about the CFA Program that they wish they'd known earlier. As a candidate, knowing these realities now can be big help.

One of my late discoveries related to why some topics seemed more difficult than others. When I left my Level II exam, I remember thinking, "The Equities, Fixed Income, and Derivatives topics didn't seem too difficult, but man those Quantitative Methods and Financial Reporting/Analysis questions were doozies. Those areas must not be my strengths." Then, something funny happened in Level III; the Equities, Fixed Income, and Derivatives topics that weren't difficult last year were suddenly very difficult this year. What happened?

In each Level, you'll find that some topics are harder than others, and you'll assume that you just aren't gifted in those areas. You might discover after taking all three exams that, in retrospect, it wasn't you. Certain topics are more difficult in certain Levels for a reason.

Topics like to go out with a bang. Not all topics are included in every Level—some are retired as the Program progresses. If you're seeing a subject for the last time, you're seeing it at its hardest. This helps explain why many candidates find topics like Quantitative Methods to be the hardest ones on the Level II exam; they won't appear next year according to the CFA Institute's topic outline for each Level. Knowing this, you can be better prepared for your Level by understanding the proficiency expected of you in each topic and putting additional effort where it's most needed.

The retiring topics may not be the largest. Candidates often focus more study time on the largest subjects, which makes sense as they influence your total score more than the rest. These big topics can also be overwhelming because they are so expansive. Like the retiring topics, they deserve lots of attention.

To determine which topics might be the most challenging whether due to retirement or size (or both), you first need to know which topics will appear on each test.

What You Can Expect to See on Each Exam

The CFA Institute publishes a matrix of testing topics and weights. This matrix explains how much of the exam will likely be concentrated in each topic. The 2014 chart is reprinted here. Be sure to look up the current matrix on the CFA Institute's website.[11]

CFA Exam Topic Area Weights

Topic Area	Level I	Level II	Level III
Ethical and Professional Standards (% of total)	*15*	*10*	*10*
Investment Tools	*50*	*30-60*	*0*
Corporate Finance	8	5-15	0
Economics*	10	5-10	0
Financial Reporting and Analysis	20	15-25	0
Quantitative Methods	12	5-10	0
Asset Classes	*30*	*35-75*	*35-45*
Alternative Investments	3	5-15	5-15
Derivatives	5	5-15	5-15
Equity Investments	10	20-30	5-15
Fixed Income	12	5-15	10-20
Portfolio Management and Wealth Planning	*5*	*5-15*	*45-55*
Total (%)	*100*	*100*	*100*

*Economics is part of Portfolio Management at Level III.
Source: CFA Institute, 2013-2014.

As can be seen in this chart, there are four chief topic collections:

1) Ethical and Professional Standards
2) Investment Tools
3) Asset Classes
4) Portfolio Management and Wealth Planning

The CFA Institute offers this matrix as a precious hint of where to focus your study hours. For example, the matrix suggests that the Investment Tools are expected to represent approximately

50 percent of the Level I test. Four topics make up this large area: (1) Corporate Finance, (2) Economics, (3) Financial Reporting and Analysis, and (4) Quantitative Methods. The CFA Institute suggests that these four topics will represent 8, 10, 20, and 12 percent of the test questions, respectively, for a total of 50 percent.

The matrix may emphasize some topics over others, but candidates shouldn't jump to the conclusion that they can ignore the smaller topics. The matrix is the starting point for building a winning study strategy, but it's not the final authority on the matter. Don't only hit the large subjects and consider yourself safe. Smaller topics might show up in a big way this year, or vice versa. The CFA Institute carefully and explicitly warns candidates that actual exam weights may vary from year to year (except for Ethics). This chart is not a guarantee, but simply a guide. Every topic must be reviewed, albeit some require extra attention.

More importantly, the topic matrix tells you more than topic weights. The full chart depicting the weights for Levels I, II, and III is actually a clue as to which topics will be the most challenging for your individual Level. Large topics may be time consuming, but they aren't necessarily the hardest. By looking at the structure of each Level, you can know what to expect in yours.

Level I Has Uniform Difficulty

In the topic matrix, you can see that Level I has precise topic weights without the vast ranges that you see in Levels II and III. These firmer weights give more reliable insight into how you should split your time among topics.

The heaviest Level I topic weights are Financial Reporting and Analysis (20 percent), Ethics (15 percent), Quantitative Methods (12 percent), and Fixed Income (12 percent). Approximately 60 percent of the Level I test covers these four topics, and it likely won't deviate much from these estimations. When planning your study regimen, allocate extra time to these subjects. Maybe set aside two weeks for the big topics while, for a small topic like Alternative Investments, schedule a couple of days (I explain the details of my proven study plan in Chapter 8, "A Study Plan from Start to Finish").

If you've been a fixed income analyst for the last ten years, the Fixed Income study sessions may be a breeze for you whereas others may be tougher. If you know a subject, you can limit your time spent on it but don't skip it altogether. You are learning the CFA Institute's views and methods. It's the CFA Institute's test, so you must learn its ways. No matter your familiarity, cover every topic.

Since Level I is a foundation course, no single subject seems to challenge candidates more than any other. Most candidates cite Ethics as the hardest subject at Level I, but I believe this is due to rampant underestimation of the subject's trickiness and, thus, lack of adequate preparation. Overall, count on consistent difficulty between subjects as you study for this exam. Level I shouldn't present enormous challenges if you put in the time.

Levels II and III Are Different Stories

A frightening event happens after you pass the Level I test and register for the next: Your Level II curriculum books arrive. Soon enough, you will realize that you're in way over your head. Every sensible candidate has this feeling at some point during the Level II process. It doesn't matter if you've been in the industry for decades; the concepts may be familiar, but the details drown everyone.

You have moved beyond basic training. The Level II test searches for the Navy Seals of Finance. The CFA Institute wants only those candidates willing to sacrifice and endure. At every turn, Level II tries to determine which candidates are both the most qualified and the most dedicated to becoming CFA charterholders.

Obviously, every topic must become more demanding than it was in Level I. This is probably not a shock, but the width of the chasm between the Levels tends to take most candidates by surprise.

Look at the Level II column in the topic matrix with all those nerve-racking ranges! As little as 30 percent of the test will cover Investment Tools, or as much as 60 percent. Somewhere between 35 and 75 percent will cover Asset Classes, which is a 40-point swing. This chart describes the reason why almost all candidates find Level II to be the most difficult. As you look for areas that may be skipped or covered lightly, there's nowhere to hide. The Institute might stress smaller topics and completely eliminate big ones; you'll find out on test day.

Though the CFA Institute provides zero indication of which topics will be more difficult in Level II, the secret lies in the third column of the table: the Level III weights. The Level III Investment Tools section shows a list of zeroes. By Level III, you're expected to know the Investment Tools and won't be tested on them. So, what do you think is going to happen in Level II, which is the Investment Tools' final assessment? Pure torture designed to weed out anyone who hasn't achieved proficiency in that area. Be an expert in the Investment Tools category for Level II.

This theory also gives insight into Level I, but in the opposite manner. If a certain section will be covered again in the next Level, the topic probably won't be the toughest it could possibly get, because that will come later. You don't have to kill yourself in Level I trying to achieve that expert level just yet. Every Level builds on the previous one, as does the intricacy of each topic. Once a topic is in its final testing stage—like the Investment Tools in Level II—this is the most demanding it's going to become.

Certain subjects clearly dominate Level II, but only some of these weighty topics won't be tested again. If the test creators lean towards the highest end of the topic ranges, you've got an enormous 55 percent of the test wrapped up in only two subjects: (1) Financial Reporting and Analysis and (2) Equity Investments. Be aware that Financial Reporting and Analysis won't be covered again in Level III. Because this is the last time that Financial Reporting and Analysis will be tested and it is so large, this topic tends to be the most brutal for Level II candidates.

Graduating to Level III brings a much needed change of pace, as the test gravitates to more qualitative concerns. Still, there's little comfort here. Again, you will encounter an exam that ensures proficiency, but this time in every topic. All topics are at their most difficult, so it's a demanding test. By now though, you really know what finance is all about. You also know your weaknesses, your strengths, and the ideal study regimen. Every candidate has his or her opinions about the relative difficulty of each subject in Level III, which tend to reflect each person's predilection for some topics over others. By Level III, we learn to battle our weaknesses and force the arduous subjects into submission.

For me, Level III was the most enjoyable Level. Computer programs can calculate equations for us, but the qualitative concepts in Level III require a human mind.

Many candidates cite Level III as the easiest Level overall, and these are the candidates who take the essay format in stride. Unlike the previous two Levels, which are all multiple-choice, half of the Level III exam consists of essay questions and the other half consists of multiple choice questions. On the essay questions, there are no answer choices to pick from or options to jog your memory. Every list, equation, and definition must come to mind in seconds and then be communicated in written English under a tremendous time crunch. It is the test structure that defeats candidates in Level III rather than any specific subject.

Level III is more about garnering polish and sophistication across the asset classes and circumstances you may find in your daily work. There's little need for a topic matrix in Level III; it blends the subjects into a comprehensive test.

How the Tests Are Graded

A 70 percent has always achieved a passing result on the CFA exams.[12] However, that's not the whole story (as usual). It seems that the CFA Institute often sets a passing rate substantially below 70 percent because so few candidates achieve that target. This isn't done ahead of time; there's not a predetermined passing score on any of the CFA exams. Instead, the powers that be wait to compare the candidates' performance to each other in determining a passing grade. You're judged against all other candidates taking the same exam as well as the proficiency levels of candidates on prior exams. Essentially, the test is curved.

Also a consideration, in standard-setting workshops, groups of CFA charterholders give their assessments of how a qualified candidate would answer each question of the exam. The CFA Institute Board of Governors is ultimately responsible for choosing a minimum passing score (MPS) and, in doing so, takes into account the results from the standard setting workshops, the difficulty of the exam, and overall candidate performance. Performance on the ethics questions may also be taken into account in arriving at a final list of passing candidates. The CFA Institute states, "The Board's objective [with this process] is to set a consistent standard competency level across years."[13]

The Institute never releases the minimum passing score for any exam nor informs candidates of their scores. You will receive a "pass" or "fail" result, not a numerical grade.

As insight into your pass or fail result, the CFA Institute informs you of how many of the available points you got correct in each topic area: less than 50 percent, 50 to 70 percent, or more than 70 percent. Generally, you need to earn more than 70 percent of the available points on most topics to gain a passing score with minimal below-50 percent results on the other topics.

I'm frequently asked if candidates ever receive an overall passing result while scoring less than 50 percent in a topic. Yes, this is possible. In Level II, I scored less than 50 percent in two topics: the largest (Financial Reporting and Analysis) and one of the smallest (Alternative Investments). I admit that I was surprised by the difficulty of the Financial Reporting and Analysis topic—had I known the lesson that retiring topics tend to be extra difficult, I would have expected this and prepared accordingly. Still, with greater than 70 percent performance in all other topics, I passed. This demonstrates that an effective study regimen in every topic can help achieve a passing score despite weak spots.

My Level III performance followed a similar pattern. I received less than 50 percent of the available points on one essay question and one item set (both related to Portfolio Management). I scored well on the rest of the exam, including seven other Portfolio Management areas, and passed.

In explaining outcomes like these, the CFA Institute's website notes, "You do not need to achieve a minimum score in any topic area. The pass/fail result is based solely on the total points you score on the exam compared with the minimum passing score (MPS) established by the CFA Institute Board of Governors for each exam. The only exception to this rule is a [possible] 'Ethics adjustment.'"[14] (Ethics is discussed further in the next chapter.)

Knowing that you can feasibly earn less than 50 percent of the points in a topic and pass the exam is not a reason to forsake any subject. You should prepare for every topic. Candidates typically have weaknesses, some of which may be heightened by the fact that a topic is large or retiring (such as the Financial Reporting and Analysis topic from my Level II exam). By scoring well in the other areas, you can earn a passing result.

With the CFA Institute's process for determining a minimum passing score, you can't know what the MPS is before test day. It is shaped by that particular exam and how the total candidate pool performs. I recommend thinking less about the numerical score and more about outperforming your competition. You may not know the difficulty of your particular exam ahead of time or the minimum passing score. But, considering recent passing rates, you know that average performance will not pass. Therefore, be ready to outperform. Surpass the average study routine. In Part 2, "Study Regimen," I'll describe how to prepare in an above-average way.

Mind the Big, Retiring Topics

As you think about the Level you're attempting and review the topic matrix, make sure you consider both size and finality for each topic. These two characteristics should determine where you expend the most study effort.

The topics that extend for hundreds of pages are challenging if for no other reason than the fear that they may never end. These also have a bigger influence on your results, so give them extra attention.

The topics that won't be making a reappearance at the next Level are often the most difficult. If you're seeing a topic for the last time, expect testing agony and study accordingly. For topics that are both large and retiring, well, study even more.

The topic matrix is a useful tool, but make sure you review every topic. Don't skip a single area. While some subjects might claim more study hours than others, covering every topic is extremely important to achieving a passing score. The CFA Institute knows that some candidates try to ignore the smaller topics, and it would like to minimize this behavior. Occasionally, the CFA Institute deviates from its testing matrix in a meaningful way to remind us that we're never safe. Don't exhaust yourself trying to guard against this possibility; you can't learn each topic as if it will be the star of the show. However, cover each topic as if it will receive some representation on the test, because it likely will.

Key Takeaways: The Second Secret to Passing CFA Exams

- The CFA Institute's topic matrix explains which subjects carry heavier weights on each Level's exam.

- When a topic is making its last appearance, candidates usually find it to be one of the hardest subjects on the exam. Make sure you are fully proficient in the area.

- Some topics are more heavily weighted than others. The weightier topics have a bigger influence on your total score and, therefore, need extra attention.

- No subject may be safely omitted from your study plan. Give the larger and retiring topics more study time, but don't skip the others.

- In Level I, all topics are relatively similar in regards to difficulty. Focus on building your foundation in every topic.

- In Level II, consider that many subjects will be retired afterwards and not covered again. These topics will likely pose the biggest challenges.

- In Level III, the test ensures proficiency in all remaining areas, so it is a difficult exam. Often, though, the test's structure defeats candidates rather than any specific subject.

- The CFA Institute has historically passed all candidates scoring 70 percent or higher but may set a lower minimum passing score. You need to score above 70 percent in most subjects to clench a passing outcome.

CHAPTER 5

What Ethics Is Really All About

All candidates complain about studying. We complain to ourselves. We complain to each other. We complain to friends, families, and strangers in the grocery line. We complain through internet forums and social media websites. We occasionally succumb to melodrama and complain to the universe at large. But, somehow, even with eighteen study sessions to choose from, one subject unites us in collective frustration: Almost everyone's favorite subject to complain about is Ethics.

Ethics is a major focus in the CFA Program, which stems from the CFA Institute's adopted mission of promoting the financial industry's ethics. Its website, emails, social media posts, and every other communication medium drill the topic every day. The financial industry has been seriously injured by ethical scandals, and having this message in our industry is important. I generally think the CFA Program's ethics focus is a good thing.

However, the Institute's ethics rules are highly complex. The Ethics study session is usually one of the most challenging in every stage of the CFA Program.

Most candidates are in the CFA Program for about five minutes before someone warns them about the tough Ethics topic. You might be hoping to find out what makes the subject so difficult. It's more than just a "challenging subject." Ethics is always intricate, often counterintuitive, and occasionally weird. There are ways to study it and ways not to.

Candidates devise various methods for minimizing the Ethics pain. You would be amazed at how many candidates ask me if Ethics can simply be skipped altogether.

"The Ethics material is so boring," they say. "I hate studying it. Can I just skip Ethics and still pass? It feels like torture, and I really can't take it."

Yes, the Ethics study session can be frustrating, but it's not torture. Try to maintain some perspective, even on those days that lead to complaining to the universe at large. Moreover, learning the Ethics material is a key secret to passing the CFA tests.

The Ethics study session is about 200 pages of material versus other subjects that are 500 or more. With this smaller size, you can absorb every word slowly and completely, which results in correct answers on test day. This opportunity won't present itself in the other study sessions.

Secondly, this topic has enough heft to make you want to get the questions right. Ethics makes up 15 percent of the Level I exam and 10 percent of the Level II and III exams, all of which are difficult enough to pass already. These small percentages may not sound like much, but consider that severely failing this section of the test will necessitate passing every other subject with flying colors. You would begin from an 85 or 90 percent starting point rather than 100 percent. Failing the Ethics portion results in zero room for error.

Beside the fact that Ethics comprises a significant portion of these exams, another major reason to give Ethics its due respect is the method by which the CFA Institute handles candidates that score in a narrow range around the minimum passing score (MPS). If your total exam score barely misses the MPS but you manage to pass Ethics, you may be bumped up to a passing result. Conversely, if you're on the line and also fail Ethics, you may be moved into the failing category, even if you would have otherwise barely passed.

Consider what this means: you can fail the test and still end up with a passing score, if you pass Ethics. That should be a huge incentive to learn this topic. As another incentive, you might achieve the total passing score and end up failing anyway because you failed Ethics. Don't chance it.

Look on the Bright Side

Within the convoluted Ethics material lies a precious gift: certainty of the topic's size, weight, and difficulty.

Its size is substantial. The topic is pretty large with 10 to 15 percent weights. And, it's difficult. How is any of this good news? Well, certainty is a precious commodity in the CFA Program. More certainty increases your chance of a passing score because you know what's coming.

Ethics is the only subject in the CFA curriculum that gives any sense of certainty. The Ethics weights are not estimations; they are set in stone. In Level I, you can know without a doubt that 36 questions out of the total 240 will come from this relatively small section of the curriculum. These points cannot be left on the table, because the other subjects won't provide such certainty. You'll have no way of knowing which parts of these other sprawling curriculum books will make it onto the test. Granted, you can't know which parts of the Ethics session will make it onto the test either but, with less material, you can cover every page with a keen eye.

Additionally, at least by Level II, candidates encounter a few obscure, unrecognizable questions throughout the non-Ethics portion of the test. Such questions test you on concepts that were buried deep in the curriculum and mentioned, almost fleetingly, in a couple of short paragraphs. Ethics points can save you from obscure questions like these that the CFA Institute throws on every test. You might miss those questions, but your performance on Ethics can offset them. Know Ethics. Really know it.

Why the Ethics Topic Is so Exasperating

Here's the especially frustrating thing about Ethics: No matter how hard you study, you will walk out of the test wondering if you failed that section. The Ethics questions are notoriously tricky. The CFA-test makers seem to purposefully write hazy, it-could-go-either-way questions to make you squirm.

Believe me, I feel your frustration. Ethics is vexing for many reasons, not least of which is the subject's arbitrary, subjective nature.

Often the line is quite thin between a CFA ethics violation and a passable business practice. For example, when leaving an employer, it's a serious violation to copy and take an internal client contact list because it's confidential information that you might use to steal the employer's clients. Instead, if you find each customer's contact information through public or other means, feel free to take every one of your employer's clients.[15] The actual taking of the clients is irrelevant: the CFA Institute cares how you do it.

As another example, the Institute expects candidates and charterholders to maintain objectivity when performing investment research for clients. To this end, you are encouraged to decline paid transportation and lodging when visiting companies that you are researching. However, if commercial transportation is not convenient for the location or itinerary, you can ride on the company's corporate jet and stay—expenses paid—in a nearby hotel, as long as it is "modest."

Would you answer questions about these scenarios correctly? The Ethics topic is full of specific situations like these. To score well in Ethics, you need to know the CFA Institute's intricacies that, at times, will drive you mad.

Because of these nuances, after each test I had no idea if I completely bombed Ethics or conquered it. Yet, if you're prepared, you'll score well. In each Level, I scored better than 70 percent in Ethics because I was prepared. If nothing else, the CFA Institute is very good at separating those who studied from those who didn't in each subject, and Ethics is no different.

The Ethics questions on the tests are tough so you'll internalize the rules. The material stays burned in your brain long after the exams, which is exactly the CFA Institute's intention. Most of the rules are reasonable and indispensable, like the requirement to exercise prudent judgment when investing client money. Some are not. All are potential test questions.

The jargon I use in this book is required by the CFA Institute's code of conduct and is fair game on test day. CFA-test takers are to be referred to as CFA candidates. We are only to use the term "CFA" as an adjective, never a noun. Stating that someone is a "CFA charterholder" is acceptable, while stating the same person is a "CFA" is not.

This drives most CFA charterholders crazy, including me. Obviously, a chartered person is *by definition* a charterholder. The rule that I must refer to myself as a "CFA charterholder" is grammatically incorrect and bizarre, considering the term is short for "Chartered Financial Analyst charterholder." The CFA Institute doesn't acknowledge that phrase's redundancy or improper use of English, which is ironic considering Chapter 3's discussion about how you're expected to know fluent English for the exams. In my day-to-day work, I'm consistently met with raised eyebrows as people wonder why I refer to myself as a chartered charterholder. If you complete the CFA Program, you'll be welcomed into a shared joke in which we all roll our eyes as we describe ourselves as "CFA charterholders" to satisfy the ethics rules.

The Ethics study session declares how the designation should appear after your name, as well. Take a look at my name on the front cover of this book. Notice that my name and the letters "CFA" share the same font size and style. I'm welcome to put "CFA" after my name, but "CFA" can't be more prominently displayed with bolder or larger font.

To explain these rules, I didn't have to pull out my study materials to refresh my memory; the CFA exams ensured that I'll never forget them.

As you study the Ethics topic, you might come across rules that seem to be a tad overreaching and illogical. They are drastically outnumbered by vital rules in the Ethics material that our industry so desperately needs to follow, such as the callings to disclose conflicts of interest, maintain professionalism, and uphold the integrity of capital markets. Most of the Ethics guidelines are very appropriate.

Regardless of your opinion on the merit of each rule, you must learn all of them. The smallest guideline may be fashioned into an exam question. Moreover, the CFA Institute makes the rules and grants the CFA charter, so you have to abide by its rules or risk consequences.

It is a violation of the CFA Institute's standards to disobey any of the Ethics rules in spoken or written word. I'm required to abide by every guideline if I want to keep my charter. The CFA Institute can (and occasionally does) revoke charters in response to serious violations. While the CFA Institute probably wouldn't revoke a charter for a small infraction such as improper reference to the CFA designation, it revokes charters for worse offenses. Revoking doesn't occur privately; in very public fashion, the CFA Institute publishes your name and violation online and in its global publication for all the world to see.

The CFA Institute also disciplines a number of candidates due to exam-related violations every year. In recent years, more than 200 candidates had their exam results voided due to violations including receiving or giving assistance during the exam, writing past time is called, opening the question booklet before the exam began, and using unauthorized scratch paper. The worst offenders were given lengthy suspensions from the CFA Program, with 70 candidates permanently barred from participating in the CFA Program.[16]

The CFA Institute isn't kidding about this ethics stuff. It takes the rules seriously, and the exams will, too.

The Ethics Study Materials

Two pieces of work make up the Ethics portion of the curriculum; candidates receive both as part of their curriculum book set. First, the two-page pamphlet *Code of Ethics & Standards of Professional Conduct (Code and Standards)* provides overarching principles by which all CFA candidates and charterholders must abide. Every word of these two pages should be memorized.

To support the *Code and Standards*, the CFA Institute publishes a handbook to guide the application of the principles in daily, professional life. This is the *Standards of Practice Handbook*, which is roughly 200 pages long. Think of this handbook as your survival guide. It contains the answer to every Level I and II Ethics test question (Level III includes an additional handbook related to asset management called the *Asset Manager Code of Professional Conduct*).

Ethics is the only topic that has the same study material for Level II as it did for Level I, and it's blessedly short (relative to other study sessions). You should review it closely and compulsively.

Skip the Curriculum's Ethics Cases

In addition to the *Code and Standards* and the *Standards of Practice Handbook*, the curriculum books also contain Ethics cases, which are basically long examples of the Ethics principles in practice. These lengthy cases are diversions because, right now, you are short on time and need to be focused on high-impact study activities. For the exam, I recommend skipping the cases. The background material is worth reviewing for your career (later), but the cases provide no new testable information. They merely repeat the *Code and Standards* and the *Standards of Practice Handbook* in story form. Reading them is not a good use of your study time.

The cases also don't match the exams' structures. In Level I, the test questions are in stand-alone, multiple-choice format without a vignette or story, so don't waste time learning how to deconstruct cases like you're in business school. I watched my husband learn this skill for his MBA classes, and it didn't look easy!

Even in Levels II and III, which do present miniature ethics cases on the exams, you're better off answering practice questions that more closely resemble the real deal. In these Levels, the test presents a short narrative of ethical quandaries, followed by some multiple choice questions about the narrative you just read. This is very different from the long, elaborate ethics cases in the curriculum books that contain obvious ethics infractions that don't challenge your understanding of the material. My advice is to spend your study time on tasks that add more value rather than reviewing cases that bear little resemblance to the CFA exams.

Establishing an Ethics Strategy

To learn Ethics, tackle this topic early in your study plan and return to it often.

I suggest one of two approaches depending on your study preference. First, you could read through the *Code and Standards* and the longer *Standards of Practice Handbook* at least two or three times in succession and complete all practice problems (don't forget the asset management handbook in Level III). Highlight all key points in the body of the handbooks and within practice questions. By the end of this process, more than 50 percent of your materials should be highlighted because almost every paragraph and practice question contains key points. Even short phrases sometimes establish new rules or exceptions that can become a test question. With the Ethics topic, you can't be too detail oriented.

Every few weeks throughout your study months, return to your highlighted resources and review them again. I was able to fit this task in to my otherwise full study schedule by making it a part of my normal, personal routine. I like to read before I go to sleep at night; every few weeks, for several nights, I would supplant the Ethics booklets for my bedtime reading material.

If highlighting the CFA Institute's Ethics material is not your favorite idea, you can rely more heavily on study notes and less on the CFA Institute-provided handbooks. Candidates can obtain a set of Ethics study notes from a third-party vendor. There are a number of such test prep providers, which can be found with an internet search for "CFA study notes" or by referring to the "Test Preparation Resources" section in the back of this book, where I've listed many providers and described each.

For the Ethics study session, relying *only* on the third-party study notes is a risky strategy. Using both, though, gives the benefit of new perspectives. I used the CFA Institute's materials and the third-party study notes, which let me learn the guidelines from more than one angle. Ethics is the one part of the curriculum that I never replaced with study notes because the Ethics test questions are so particular. But only you know how best you learn.

Whichever route you take—leaning on the CFA Institute's material or the third-party notes—attempt at least 100 practice questions as you study Ethics. Practice questions uncover your true understanding of the information. The *Standards of Practice Handbook* comes with dozens of solid practice questions; answer them. The CFA Institute also introduced practice quizzes for each topic in the 2014 exam cycle. Finally, third-party Ethics questions are also generally challenging and resemble those seen on recent CFA exams. You can purchase access to these practice questions, some of which are very affordable. (Again, you can check the "Test Preparation Resources" for more information.)

The questions on test day will obviously differ from practice examples, but you'll be prepared to answer the given exam question. There is only so much finagling and trickiness that the CFA Institute can do with 200 pages of material, so it's likely that the test day questions will resemble your practice questions.

Know Ethics to Boost Your Total Score

I cannot stress this enough: know Ethics. It's not going to be fun, but knowing Ethics is a straightforward secret to passing the CFA Program. The material is relatively short and the number of related questions is relatively high. You know exactly how many Ethics questions appear on the exam; let this certainty help your total score. Also critical, the CFA Institute will present you with a failing score if you're skirting the line and also fail the Ethics section on test day.

These questions yield vital points that tend to have a significant influence regarding who appears on the passing list and who does not. Plus, you will want to know the rules so you can actually keep your charter once you earn it!

Key Takeaways: What Ethics Is Really All About

- The Ethics topic makes up 15 percent of the Level I test and 10 percent of the Level II and III tests, which are substantial weights.

- If your total exam score is within a narrow range of the minimum passing score, your overall result may be changed based on your performance in Ethics.

- The answer to every Ethics exam question in Levels I and II can be found in the two-page *Code of Ethics & Standards of Professional Conduct (Code and Standards)* or the roughly 200-page *Standards of Practice Handbook*; both will be included in your curriculum books. Level III also tests candidates on the *Asset Manager Code of Professional Conduct*.

- Your study plan should introduce the Ethics material early and often. Review it again every few weeks until test day.

- The curriculum books' Ethics cases are not particularly helpful for the exam; focus study hours on the main *Code and Standards* and the *Standards of Practice Handbook*.

- To learn Ethics, read the CFA Institute materials a couple of times in succession and complete 100 practice questions. Review these materials every few weeks during your study months. Or, use both the CFA Institute materials and third-party study notes.

- Complete at least 100 practice questions as you learn the Ethics material. If possible, review both examples from the

Standards of Practice Handbook and practice questions from a third-party resource.

- Ethics is an extremely nuanced topic. One short sentence from the CFA Institute's materials can become a full-blown test question. Study Ethics closely and know every rule intimately.

CHAPTER 6

A Quiet, Important Statistic

I am usually a sunny person, but I must be a gloomy black cloud for a few pages. The CFA Program's failure rate is an incredibly important statistic that is rarely discussed in terms of the full Program. I admit that this is not a particularly fun topic for discussion. But soon you will move on to establishing a study regimen, and the odds of failing should remain top of mind as you craft the perfect plan to overcome the miserable odds. Like an Olympian who knows that very few people make it through trials, use the information in this chapter to propel your CFA training.

The probability of failing is quite high. I don't mean that lots of people fail, so you should study hard. I mean almost everyone— approximately 92 percent—never make it through the CFA Program.[17] Inversely, only eight percent see their CFA charterholder dreams realized. Eight percent. Studying hard is a quaint concept in the face of these numbers.

How can the overall passing rate be so miniscule? After all, recent passing rates have been roughly 40 percent for Levels I and II, followed by a cheery 50 percent success rate for Level III. At first glance, I concede that the 92 percent failing ratio looks like a fabrication.

We must consider that the CFA tests are completed in order. Like a mathematical permutation (which is a concept you'll briefly cover in Level I), completing a series of tasks *in order* drastically reduces the number of successes at the end. This aspect of the CFA Program is what produces such low overall passing rates.

The Odds Are Against You

Contemplate the following example (and bear with me while I throw a bunch of numbers at you). Let's consider the typical passing rates of 40 percent, 40 percent, and 50 percent for the Level I, Level II, and Level III tests, respectively. Say you sit for the Level I test with 100,000 fellow candidates, which is roughly the number of candidates who sat for the Level I exam in June, 2013. Applying a 40 percent passing rate results in 40,000 triumphant candidates who move on to Level II. Conversely, 65,000 candidates just saw their plans for becoming CFA charterholders become postponed or terminated.

Next year, Level II removes tens of thousands more from the passing list with another low success rate of 40 percent. We're now down to 12,250 candidates attempting Level III. That test will remove many more, and we arrive at a final charterholder-worthy group of 6,125. This number represents a six percent passing rate out of the 100,000 people who started the journey with you. Add in the dedicated candidates who retake failed exams, and the total passing rate is roughly eight percent.

This hypothetical example is backed up by the real numbers. In the decade of 2004 through 2013, only 97,707 candidates passed all three Levels compared to 1.3 *million* people who started the Program.[18] This is a very low success rate that, you guessed it, equals eight percent.

The failure rate can be a bit of a bummer. To dampen your mood further, we must also consider how the tests become more difficult with each new Level.

Each time tens of thousands of candidates are eliminated from the pool of contenders, the Program becomes more challenging. You're competing against more capable competition, so the CFA Institute must raise the bar.

In my earlier example, Level I didn't only eliminate 65,000 candidates. It eliminated 65,000 people you'd much rather test against than the 35,000 candidates you're left with. After all, those 35,000 candidates just demonstrated that they know what they're doing. This necessitates increasing the difficulty of the Level II test since the surviving candidates have demonstrated that they can handle the difficulty of Level I. Therefore, the degree of comprehension that secured a passing Level I score last year may not be enough for a passing Level II score this year.

Because of this weeding out process, there are very few CFA charterholders on the planet. I am the 124,558[th] person to ever receive the CFA charter, which was granted to me in September, 2011. Each charter is awarded with a sequential number, which is how I know my place in line. This means that since 1963, the year the CFA charter was launched, only 124,557 people succeeded in this program before me.

To put the number of CFA charterholders in perspective, consider this: more people will sit for the upcoming June tests—

one single day's tests—than have earned the charter in fifty years. Fifty years!

I'll be honest with you. Knowing these realities and statistics, I doubt I would have started the CFA Program. I'm certainly glad that I completed the Program, but this is easy for me to say now. If I had sunk years of my life into a certification that continued to evade me—years that could have been spent obtaining a guaranteed master's degree or a faster certificate—I doubt I would feel the same way. I still recommend entering the CFA Program; there is value in passing any of the Levels and, with a solid study routine, you can pass all three. But I also recommend entering with eyes wide open.

Sit with the statistics for a while. The dismal odds of failing reveal that the Program is about dedication, not intelligence. Reflect on how much you want the CFA charter, and what you're willing to do to earn it.

If you start this program, do what is necessary to count yourself among the approximate eight percent of successful candidates. Commit to passing. Realize that passing all three Levels in succession will require uncommon focus that 92 percent of candidates cannot sustain.

Use the cost of failing as motivation to put in a few extra hours each week. The cost of failing a Level is higher than any other program of which I know. Yet another year of your life must be sacrificed. Months of studying are wasted with no CFA letters to show for it. You must wait to retake a test that is only given once a year (at Levels II and III) and carries no guarantee next time, either. Perhaps a raise or promotion is lost. Pay the hefty test fees—again. Watch the day when your social life can return to its former glory fade further away.

However, if you do fail a Level, first know that you have company. In fact, most candidates failed with you. Next, decide if you'll stick with the Program or not. To make this decision, understand why you failed and by how much. Also consider which Level you're attempting, since the Level should be a helpful factor as you decide what to do next. Failing Level I does not mean the same thing as failing Levels II or III, and your choices should reflect that reality.

Failing Level I Is a Bad Omen

If you fail Level I, consider quitting. Remember this is the first of three Levels. You may squeeze by next time, but Level II will be waiting. Then you will be competing against people who passed Level I with flying colors on a test that challenges finance professors with PhDs. Use your Level I scores as an indicator of how you will perform in the rest of the Program. If you know you didn't study enough—perhaps a life event disrupted your plans—try again. But if you gave it an honest shot and still failed, consider applying to a different certification.

Maybe this program simply isn't your thing. When I was in college, I thought I wanted to major in architecture. I quickly found out that architecture involves locking yourself in a room and drawing pictures of bathrooms for days on end. Besides being painfully boring, I also had no talent for it. I've never drawn a picture without my intended audience asking, "What is that?" I could hear the business school calling, and I was out of there. I moved on without much harm done. With only a few months of effort applied to the CFA Program through Level I, you can as well.

Don't fret that you've wasted your time if you resign from the Program. Level I can be a good learning experience whether you fail or not. It will give you an unparalleled foundation in finance that will serve you for the rest of your career. You'll still walk away with that foundation.

Some candidates have no intention of finishing. Perhaps earning the charter isn't your goal. Maybe you want to gain financial knowledge on your own time, and the CFA Level I curriculum appeals to you. If you pass, you've got something to put on your résumé and possibly a bargaining chip for a raise. Employers respect a candidate that finishes any Level, even if you

have no desire to finish the Program. And if you don't pass, you still learned something.

However, if you feel confident that next year (and Level II and III) will be different, use the CFA Institute-provided performance matrix to determine which subjects gave you trouble as you craft a strategy to try again. The performance matrix is emailed to each candidate with their failing score, and it gives a performance breakdown for each testing subject.

The Institute will rank your performance against everyone else who failed, and then divide the group into ten bands. For example, you may find that your total score placed you in "band 10," which means you were very close to the minimum passing score. As a band 10 candidate, you scored in the top 10 percent of the failing candidates. On the other end of the spectrum, failing in band one means a candidate was in the bottom 10 percent. Band two equates to scoring in the bottom 20 percent, and so on.

Also use your topic performance matrix which, as I discussed previously, reveals if you correctly answered less than 50 percent, 50 to 70, or more than 70 percent of the topic's questions. For example, you may find that you scored well in Quantitative Methods, but below 50 percent in Equity Investments. For the topics that gave you trouble, do something different this time around. If you struggled with the math problems, do more examples. If conceptual questions tripped you up, consider attending a lecture study course. Give the challenging areas extra attention for your next try, but also be sure to cover every topic again since the exam changes every year.

Your Level I performance matrix will point to a clear verdict as to whether or not you should quit the Program or continue on with a second attempt. Learning from your mistakes can make a big difference as you climb this mountain. But, sometimes, you're just not meant to climb above base camp. You'll know which option applies to you.

In Level II, Misery Loves Company

Based on my unscientific research, failing Level II is common among people who now have CFA charters hanging on their walls. I cleared Level II on my first attempt, but not before I scored below 50 percent on the largest portion of the test.

Many people face a difficult decision after they receive their Level II scores. Fail Level II and the question becomes, "What now?" Should you try again, not wanting the previous Level and efforts to go to waste? Or cut your losses and quit?

The performance matrix and becomes even more important at Level II. The CFA Institute will again divide the failing scores in to bands and tell you where you stand. If you perform well amongst the failing candidates, try again next year. I would have given it another shot if I had barely failed. Thankfully, I saved my own behind by studying hard enough in the other sections to make up for failing the largest segment of the test. It could have gone the other way. Many people fail Level II and go on to finish the Program.

However, if you scored near the bottom of the pack (bands one through five), consider pursuing a different credential. Quitting at this point can feel like a premature defeat, but I have seen friends persist in Level II for years as they refuse to see the reality that this designation is not for them. They could have spent these years successfully pouring their efforts into work performance or another credential. Be fair to yourself by being honest with yourself.

Level II is a frustrating Level to fail. But, again, let your performance matrix and band guide you.

To Fail Level III Is to Truly Understand Disappointment

I imagine that failing Level III goes beyond frustrating; it's heart wrenching. You're so close. Your charter was practically in the mail. Instead, after everything you've sacrificed to this point, the CFA Program will claim another year of your life. Ugh.

My advice for Level III is different than the previous two Levels and unequivocal: Finish. Do whatever it takes. Your odds of passing next year are relatively decent based on recent Level III pass rates of approximately 50 percent. You also now have experience with the dreaded essay format of the morning session, which next year's new Level III candidates will experience for the first time. Factoring in these candidates, your passing odds are more like 60/40 rather than 50/50. Make some adjustments and attack next year's test.

Don't let the last two years of exertion (or more) go to waste. If English is not your first language and thus the Level III essay questions are difficult for you, practice English this fall by writing in a journal each day. Perhaps take an advanced English class.

If you thought the test questions were complicated and tricky, start studying earlier this year. Just get through it. I would even suggest taking the test a third time if you fail again. The monetary and professional rewards of a CFA charter can be large, and all you need is a test that lets you squeak out a pass.

Failure Is Likely, but That's a Good Thing

Alas, failing at least one of the CFA exams is very possible. I won't pat you on the back and say there's no shame in failing. Of course there's shame in failing. Finance is our profession, and failing a test that measures your financial knowledge is an embarrassing event. But I also commend your bravery in signing up knowing that you may have to go into your workplace in nine months and admit failure. In a world where everyone gets a trophy (well, at least in the Unites States), the CFA Program refuses to give us one just because failing makes us feel bad. I love that.

This program doesn't care how much you want it. As long as you can pay the test fees, it doesn't care how much money you have. Your social status is irrelevant, as are any previous accomplishments. It only cares that you fulfill the same requirements that apply to everyone else. The industry can thus be assured that the charterholders are the financial elite, not people whose money, surname, or other supplement for actual ability got them to where they are. Professionally, few experiences will compare to the pride you feel when someone says, "Wow, you are a CFA charterholder?" The Program's low passing rates maintain this high regard for the designation.

It's a dreary reality of the CFA Program that most everyone fails. However, that truth makes the charter so valuable. If you succeed in the CFA Program, you will have achieved something truly rare. It's not easy to stand out in today's employment landscape, but these three letters do.

Key Takeaways: A Quiet, Important Statistic

- The overall passing rate for the full CFA Program is approximately eight percent. Almost everyone will fail.

- Less than 200,000 people have been granted the CFA charter since the designation's founding in 1963. Comparatively, about 200,000 people will take the CFA exams this year alone.

- The Program becomes more difficult with each passing Level because candidates are weeded out along the way. As your competition becomes more adept, you need to increase your command of the curriculum, too.

- If you fail Level I, consider quitting. The CFA designation simply may not be your calling. The next two Levels are more difficult and your Level I scores should inform your expectations for the rest of the Program.

- Failing Level II comes with a difficult choice. If you were close to passing, I suggest that you try again. However, failing by a wide margin might indicate that this should be the end of the road.

- If you fail Level III, there's only one option: try again. You're almost there! Find a way to finish the Program.

- One of the Program's best features is its high probability of failing. The charter is worth seeking because so few people attain it. Knowing the odds, you can prepare to become one of the successful eight percent.

PART TWO

Study Regimen

STUDY REGIMEN

Part One built a foundation for CFA-test taking success. It's time to dive into how to structure your study regimen. Keep the Part One groundwork in mind as you move forward to laying out an action plan.

Many candidates use trial and error in establishing a study regimen, which can be frustrating and costly. You need to cut through the CFA clutter and find out what regimen can lead to passing scores the first time.

As you contemplate your study plan, you may be unsure of how to piece the right study tools together into an actionable whole. You might be afraid of wasting time on things that don't add value, or even more afraid of omitting activities that make the real difference—those things that passing candidates do which set them apart.

Part Two helps you solve these problems by showing you exactly what to do and what pitfalls to avoid so you can pass these exams with confidence and efficiency. You'll learn effective methods that are consistent across all three Levels, as well as specific actions for each one. At the end, for easy reference throughout the Program, I summarize the strategies for Levels I, II, and III and include examples of week-by-week study plans.

There's no ambiguity here. With a sound study regimen, you can pass the CFA exams. Part Two explains my proven system for passing and helps you implement it.

CHAPTER 7

The 300-Hour Trap

In designing a study plan, you need to know how many hours to study. This is an important decision that is introduced early in the CFA Program.

After registering for the Level I test, your curriculum books arrive from the CFA Institute in a heavy box. The next several months will revolve around these books, which contain everything you need to know for the exam. Upon opening the box, you'll discover a typed note from the CFA Institute.

The note is jolly and upbeat. Welcome to the CFA Program! Prepare to embark on a thrilling journey! Be proud of yourself for taking this step in your career! You are surprised by your own excitement. You start envisioning "CFA" on new business cards. Previously implausible career paths flash before your eyes. You continue reading down the page and then, there it is: the CFA

Institute observes that candidates typically study at least 300 hours for each exam. That equates to a minimum of 900 total study hours across the entire CFA Program. For perspective, this is quadruple the hours recommended for a Certified Public Accountant (CPA) designation.

The CFA Program comes with a lot of studying. Perhaps this isn't news since the 300-hours-per-Level figure is trumpeted far and wide. What might be news? It's a trap.

The CFA Institute doesn't actually make a recommendation as to how many hours to study, though many test prep providers have interpreted it otherwise. Nowhere have I ever heard or read, "The CFA Institute recommends that candidates study 300 hours to pass a CFA exam." The CFA Institute does not stipulate how many hours you should study. Rather, the Institute indicates that 300 is the average number of hours that candidates report studying so you have a benchmark against which you can measure.

The 300-hour average is based on candidate surveys of those who *took* recent exams, not exclusively those who *passed*.[19] Each year, the CFA Institute asks half of the June candidates how much they studied and averages the responses—regardless if they failed or not—to arrive at 300 hours. The survey includes thousands of candidates. Both failing and passing candidates are in the response mix and, actually, more failing candidates influence the average since they represent a higher proportion of the population.

So, with this information, you know the average study time even though average candidates don't pass. Super. You're not aiming for average therefore, without isolating passing responses, the 300-hour recommendation is flawed. It doesn't tell you how much to study; it tells you exactly how much studying is not enough.

The 300-hour target may have sufficed when it was first announced, but not anymore. Generally, when candidates learn of a new average, they study more to surpass whatever that threshold is. The bar keeps rising. Case in point: not too long ago, the CFA Institute held that candidates studied 250 hours for each CFA exam. As more and more candidates studied extra to escape the middle, they established a new average of 300. Successful candidates understand that average equals failing. You must play this game, too. Since the goal is to perform above average, study more than the average candidate.

The CFA Institute needs the charter to be seen as a designation with discerning standards but still within reach; 300 hours is already asking a lot. Perhaps, the CFA Institute hesitates to publish how many hours passing candidates study because that average is probably much higher. Your jolly welcome letter will frustratingly hint at the real-time commitment by noting that *successful* candidates tend to view the 300-hour recommendation as a minimum. Take the Institute's hint.

If you want to pass comfortably, put in north of 1,300 hours in total for the CFA Program. Level I will require approximately 350 hours of study time, Level II necessitates 500 hours, and Level III entails another 450 hours. Thus, you arrive at the unpleasant total of 1,300.

These totals assume you want to pass each Level on your first try. These totals also assume you don't have a master's degree in finance. Adjust as you see fit based on your own skills and background, remembering that other candidates are right now devising study schedules with which robots would have a hard time keeping up. If you reduce the hours, do so understanding that many candidates will study more than you.

Either way, the CFA Program demands a huge chunk of time. Before starting the Program, think very carefully about the commitment that it will require. This is a masters-equivalent course and the time commitment reflects that fact.

The new proposal of 1,300 total study hours considers the differences between each CFA Level and does not assume that they all require the same effort. The proposals of 350 hours for Level I, 500 hours for Level II, and 450 hours for Level III are based on curriculum lengths, test structures, and other matters that change over the Levels.

Time Commitment in Level I

I recommend studying 350 hours for the Level I exam. To demonstrate why studying 350 hours is a better goal than 300, let's see if we can make the 300 number work (spoiler alert: it won't).

CFA-study hours are spent accomplishing three objectives; absorb everything once, review all of it again, and complete several practice exams (I'll go into the details in later chapters). To evaluate how these activities fit into the conventional 300-hour timeframe, start from the total number and subtract hours for each activity.

Begin with calculating time spent on practice tests since they have defined lengths. Each practice test is six hours long plus a couple hours to review the results. Let's assume you take four practice tests during your Level I preparation. This already eats up roughly 30 hours merely taking practice tests, which leaves 270 hours of true study time for the other two activities of learning the material and reviewing it. That's only 270 hours to cover the entire curriculum. Twice.

To remember the material, candidates need to review the curriculum two times over. They will ordinarily complete an initial study phase in the first few months followed by a second review closer to test day. This creates two rounds of studying.

The first round takes roughly 200 hours. There are 18 study sessions to learn. For each, you'll need to complete readings, examples, exercises, and flashcards (discussed in Chapter 10), all of which takes time. Each session involves hours of work.

Additionally, completing practice questions is an important endeavor, considering the Level I exam contains 240 multiple-choice questions for which you must prepare. I recommend completing about 1,500 practice questions during this initial study phase, which equates to roughly 75 questions per study session. This may sound like an exorbitant amount, however, Level I practice questions are quick, short multiple-choice questions; most can be answered in under 90 seconds. You can find practice questions in the curriculum books, topic-based quizzes on the CFA Institute website, and through a third-party provider. By answering lots of questions, you can make sure that you've practiced all the major concepts from each study session.

In Level I, a typical study session requires 10 hours to adequately cover it the first time, with some needing significantly more effort and others needing less. Therefore, 200 hours is an appropriate estimate for this study phase in Level I.

To this point, we've determined that 30 of your total study hours will be allocated to practice tests and another 200 to the first review of the material. With 230 hours spoken for, only 70 remain in the 300-hour recommendation for Level I.

You need to schedule a second review period, and these remaining hours don't allow enough time. How else will you remember the textbook you read three months ago when test day is around the corner? This is where the 300-hour recommendation falls short.

As a rule of thumb, it takes approximately 60 percent as much time to review a study session as it did to study it the first time. The second review uses this much time because, for most topics, it has been weeks since you touched them. You also need to acquire more proficiency during this second pass over the material to be ready for the exam. Considering my proposal of 200 hours for the first phase, candidates would need around 120 hours for their second review period (60 percent times 200 hours). This puts you over the 300-hour threshold by 50 hours.

Candidates persistently misjudge how much time they need for this second review phase. Remember, only 10 hours were spent on each complex, extensive study session months ago; you need considerable time to remind yourself of everything you covered back then. Alas, 300 hours do not allow sufficient opportunity for a second review, which is critical to your success.

With 350 hours, there is enough time. For Level I, 350 hours provide time to learn the material, review it a second time, and take practice tests. Plan for approximately 200 hours spent learning the material, 120 hours reviewing it again, and 30 hours completing mock exams. This totals 350 hours. (In the next chapter, I will lay out how to schedule these hours each week, as well as those for Levels II and III.)

Most candidates are not so methodical in scheduling their time. Instead, many begin Level I with a blasé attitude, thinking they will "give Level I a try and see how it goes." I admit to being one of these candidates. I had only vague knowledge of the CFA Program when my first employer kindly offered to pay my test fees for Level I. Never one to pass up free money, I signed up the next day. I assumed that if I passed, I would simply repeat the same process and time commitment at Level's II and III.

Studying commenced, and Level I was not a terrible experience. In fact, it was occasionally enjoyable. I was eager to learn, and more eager to advance my career. I was also terrified of failing. So, I put in some extra study time for a total of 450 hours.

Such a commitment was excessive for Level I. Actually, I'll go out on a limb and say it was downright overkill as I passed in the highest scoring bracket in all 10 testing topics with what seemed like an 85 percent accuracy rate. Again, these are pass/fail tests. I essentially got a "B+" on a test that doesn't care if you score a "D-," as long as it's not an "F." I could have earned a passing score with 350 to 400 study hours without stepping too close to the edge. On the contrary, I believe that I would have failed had I only studied 300 hours. You must find the time commitment that gives you an acceptable passing cushion while refraining from going overboard. Try to find a happy medium; for me, 450 hours was too hot, 300 hours was too cold, and 350 hours would have been just right.

When I received a passing score for the Level I exam, I was understandably elated and excited to move on to Level II. Had I known what hell was coming, I wouldn't have been so thrilled.

Time Commitment in Level II

Level II is the mother of all weed-out courses. It is purposefully painful so as to separate the serious finance devotees from everyone else. For a program that aims to promote the subject of finance, Level II can make you hate it.

Level II's testing format requires deeper understanding of the material. Instead of 240 questions as in Level I, the Level II test contains half as many. This lower question count makes the candidate's life harder, not easier. Each question matters more to the total score and thus becomes more costly if missed.

Practice questions are again an essential activity in Level II. However, the practice questions tend to be longer to reflect the more thorough questions you'll see on the exam, and the overall volume tends to be less than in Level I. In Level II, try answering 50 practice questions for each study session during your first pass of the curriculum, and then review these again in the last few weeks before test day.

The test format is different in Level II. Rather than the easier, standalone Level I questions, the Level II exam presents short narratives with accompanying multiple-choice questions. Each narrative presents a few paragraphs of story-like information followed by six questions related to what you just read. The CFA Institute calls these sets of prose "vignettes."

If the term "vignette" sounds like a type of flower, think of it as one covered in sharp thorns. The vignettes contain irrelevant information inserted with the intention to catch the eye of an unprepared candidate. To answer these vignette questions correctly, candidates must know the many variations of individual equations, theories, etc. For example, an equation often should be modified for specific situations; do you remember every separate version of the equation and when it is appropriate to use each one? The Level II test expects you to know these distinctions and will purposefully include information for the equation's many versions to see if you know which one to apply.

Further, an entire vignette might focus on a small, narrow concept, which means you must cover each concept as if it could be the focus of six questions on test day instead of one. Large portions of the curriculum may be absent from the Level II exam, while smaller sections could be the star theme of a whole vignette. This occurs regularly on the Level II test, so be prepared.

In the end, I studied 600 hours for Level II. However, many of these hours were spent wrestling with setbacks that could have been avoided had I known the lessons in this book (I'll discuss my biggest difficulty in Chapter 9). By learning about these pitfalls in advance, you can avoid them. Therefore, I suggest that 500 hours is a more reasonable goal.

With these 500 hours, you will accomplish the same objectives as Level I (study the material, review it again, and take practice tests), but allocate more time to the first two activities. In Level II, the first study phase takes about 300 hours, the second generally requires 175, and practice tests take 30 hours, for a total of approximately 500 hours.

The important thing to remember is that the 300-hour suggestion is impractical. I have yet to meet a single CFA charterholder who was successful with a mere 300 hours of study time at Level II, unless he or she had just finished an advanced graduate course in finance. The material is dense, but this is not necessarily the challenge. This test is all about the details. The painstaking, exhaustive, minute details. And you are expected to know all of them.

Level II expects more of its contenders. The material is nearly as long as Level I and the required proficiency is much higher. Simple mathematics dictate that the hours must increase. Scheduling 500 hours is much more appropriate than 300.

Time Commitment in Level III

After the struggle of Level II, the final one provides some respite regarding overall effort. It still requires ample time, but Level III is the most rewarding and the most pertinent to the everyday practice of finance. This can make the study time less strenuous. Also, by this point, you will be a pro at judging your necessary study time, creating a study plan, and sticking to it. The trick for Level III is to master the essay format, which is not necessarily a commitment issue.

I studied 450 hours in Level III, which was the perfect amount of time and my recommendation for you. Though perhaps more pleasant to study, the Level III exam is tough, which is why you still need to commit additional hours beyond 300. It contains both essay questions (morning session) and multiple-choice questions (afternoon session). The essay questions don't provide any help in the way of answer choices; therefore many study hours are spent memorizing lists, definitions, theories, equations, and explanations for regurgitation later. The afternoon's multiple-choice questions don't provide much relief; they follow the dangerous vignette format from Level II that you've come to adore. You'll find even fewer practice questions in Level III, but they take longer to answer. Answer about 40 questions for each study session.

Levels II and III aren't very different in terms of concept difficulty. The reason I shave off 50 hours from my Level II recommendation to arrive at 450 hours for Level III is due to the truncated length of the Level III curriculum; it is materially smaller. It may be shorter but, with no answer choices to prod your memory on the essay questions, you must know the material even more thoroughly. Studying 450 hours should establish the necessary proficiency, but with a couple hours less effort each week than you expended in Level II.

Strengthen Your Odds of Passing by Studying 1,300 Hours

There you have it: a new, realistic recommendation of 1,300 study hours across the full CFA Program. If you study only the

CFA Institute-suggested 900 hours, you have a steeply higher risk of failing. Considering that some candidates—usually the passing ones—are willing to study far more than 900 hours, you can't expect to pass with only an average amount of preparation. Always keep in mind that in the CFA Program, average performance equals a failing result.

The time commitment is probably the biggest hurdle to attaining a CFA charter. I can tell you over and over how much effort and time this program will require, but it is impossible to fully appreciate the necessary dedication until after completing it. However, on a positive note, finance professionals will wholly respect your dedication in attaining the CFA designation.

For instance, I recently attended a dinner party where I met a graduate from a top MBA program. I inquired as to whether or not he thought an MBA from his school would be worth adding to my education. His exact words were, "You already completed a very impressive post-graduate program, so you probably don't need an MBA. But if you really want it anyway, getting an MBA from my school would be a lot easier than the CFA Program."

A designation with that kind of respect is worth striving for, even if it comes with 1,300 hours of study time.

Key Takeaways: The 300-Hour Trap

- The CFA Institute mentions 300 study hours as the average that candidates commit to studying, regardless if they passed or failed. Passing candidates likely study more. In reality, none of the Levels may be comfortably passed with only 300 hours of preparation.

- To avoid flirting with the failing line, you should allocate 350 hours of study time to Level I, 500 to Level II, and 450 to Level III. Thus, the total number of study hours that I recommend for the CFA Program is 1,300.

- If you plan to give only 300 hours of study time to any Level, mentally accept that you have a higher possibility of failing. In particular, Levels II and III are extremely difficult to pass with only 300 hours.

- The Level I exam consists of 240 standalone multiple-choice questions that do not relate to a story, which is an easier testing format than Level II or III.

- The Level II test contains only 120 questions, hence each has greater consequences. The test presents short narratives (known as vignettes) that are accompanied by six multiple-choice questions. This structure is challenging as vignettes sometimes have narrow focus and often include extraneous information.

- Half of the Level III test also presents vignettes with multiple-choice questions, while the other half is comprised of essay questions. With essay questions, candidates' depth of knowledge must increase further as there are no answer choices to jog your memory.

- Candidates' time commitment is well respected and understood throughout the financial industry, increasing the value of a CFA charter. The fact that the charter requires more effort than most designations contributes to why it is worth having.

CHAPTER 8

A Study Plan from Start to Finish

Studying for the CFA Program is akin to managing a project. Project management is such a key function in the business world that many companies employ people who exclusively manage new endeavors. I've had the pleasure of knowing a few project managers (and I'm married to the best one ever, in my biased opinion). They focus on three, often opposing, project goals: (1) maintain quality, (2) finish on time, and (3) preserve order by thinking sequentially and minding the critical path.

All projects have a critical path with specific tasks that must be completed sequentially, and on time, so as not to jeopardize or delay the project. These are the critical-path tasks. The project might consist of many tasks, all of which the project manager would like to complete on time. However, there are predominant ones that cause big problems if late. Project managers don't want to move the project end date (one of their paid objectives is to meet the company's deadline), so any delay in a critical-path task results in scrambling, anxiety, and potentially cutting corners on the later tasks. These critical-path tasks stress project managers out. When one crucial phase stretches longer than scheduled, they lose sleep.

You have the same three goals in the CFA Program as those of the project manager. The quality of your studying effort matters, of course. Finish the study regimen on time, too. Meanwhile, keep your sanity by completing critical tasks on schedule (for example, don't let your first study phase bleed into the next). To find your critical-path stages, plan backwards from the project due date, which is test day. The date of the test dictates everything that comes before.

Manage the CFA Program as if it's a work-related project with a delayed payday. If you treat the study plan as you would an important assignment at work or in school with a non-negotiable due date, you'll succeed.

Choosing Your Project End Date

You first must choose what your test date will be for each Level. In Levels II and III, you don't have a choice in the matter since they're only given in June. You do, however, have a choice with the Level I test, as it is offered twice each year in June and December. When choosing between these two dates, I strongly recommend that you pick the June exam.

Here's why: Taking the Level I exam in December is risky because you can't sign up for the next Level until you receive a passing result on the last. The CFA Institute releases the December exam results in late January. Even if you sign up for Level II that same day, your curriculum books won't instantly arrive. When you finally begin studying in February, your Level II prospects aren't looking too good compared to other candidates who started studying weeks ago.

Though it seems counterintuitive, the CFA Program will likely take less time if you spread out Levels I and II, because you're more likely to pass Level II on your first try. Nothing wastes time like repeating Levels.

However, if you've taken the December exam and want to pass Level II in June, you're not doomed. You can address and mitigate the risks that are posed by this tight schedule.

When your curriculum books finally arrive, for a few weeks, study as if the test is eminent. By studying with extreme intensity, you can catch up.

Or, instead of waiting for your Level I exam results to begin studying, you can purchase a third-party study system for Level II soon after sitting for your Level I exam. You can begin learning it while you wait. However, this is exhausting. Instead of six months of studying every day, you will study for twelve months straight. Many candidates lose their motivation, and I certainly don't blame them. Consider taking a vacation or break to recharge before hitting the books again.

You might wonder if taking the December exam helps your Level II outlook because the curriculum is fresher in your mind. Level II introduces new concepts, so there is not much gained by taking the Level I and II tests back-to-back. Based on my own unscientific poll of acquaintances who took the December exam, I only found one instance of a December candidate passing Level II the next June. Most ran out of time or burnt out. In your study plan, be vigilant in protecting against both of these possibilities.

For Level I, choose a project end date that makes sense for your long-term goal of passing all three exams and becoming a

CFA charterholder. Consider taking all three exams in June or, if you take Level I in December, create a solid, vigorous plan for passing Level II.

Critical-Path Steps in CFA Preparation

After determining your Level I project end date, you can plan your study hours.

Because the CFA Program has three Levels, 18 study sessions, 10 testing topics, and other intricate aspects, planning a study regimen can seem complicated. I try to simplify in the next few pages but, because I want to give you actionable specifics, this discussion may begin to feel a bit heavy. It will get easier as you take time to digest the Program and, I promise, the next few chapters, after this one, have less numbers in them.

To begin scheduling, you should first divide your CFA-test preparation into two phases, which I touched on in the last chapter. First, candidates read the entire curriculum over a few months. Then, they review everything they just learned while taking practice tests. These two phases—an initial study phase followed by a second review—are your project's critical tasks.

How long should these phases be and when should they start? These two decisions dwarf all others you'll make while studying for the CFA exams. Over my testing years, I dedicated tremendous time and brain power to which brand of study notes to choose, the number of practice tests to take, and other important, though very specific, concerns. In fact, this book is full of such morsels. We candidates simply can't resist the continuous search, search, search for CFA-testing insights. I spent hundreds of hours studying for the CFA tests and it seemed like I spent another hundred hours searching for anything that would give me an edge.

The study tools are important. But, if you haven't scheduled enough time to utilize them, the tools won't help.

Too often, candidates arbitrarily choose start dates. "January 25th sounds good. I'll start then!" In their defense, Level I candidates don't know what to expect and, therefore, must pick a date and begin. There's a better way. You can establish a sound plan if you approach the Program as a project manager. Begin from the end date and work backwards.

Assuming that you are studying for the June exam, your project ends on the first Saturday in June. Let's say that the first Saturday falls on June 7th. In the last weeks before June 7th, you'll review the material for the second time and prepare for test day. Give yourself 45 days for this second review of the material.

The 45-day timetable is a generally accepted CFA Program rule amongst successful candidates. I don't know who first devised this timeframe, but it works. Any shorter and there's not enough time. Any longer and you peak too early.

Backing up 45 days from the hypothetical test date of June 7th lands you in mid-April. April 23rd to be exact. You would start your 45-day review phase by this date.

Now, back up further to decide when to begin your first pass through the material. This phase should be deeper and slower, so you need more time. You are also balancing two objectives for this time period. First, ensure that you finish the first pass of material with 45 days to spare before test day (in our example, April 23rd). Equally important, ensure you don't burn out because you started too early.

Use the study sessions' lengths and the topic weighting matrix from Chapter 4, "The Second Secret to Passing CFA Exams," to guide your decision. I've reprinted the matrix here for reference, which indicates which topics will likely take more time. However, you can't know until you see the curriculum books exactly how long each study session is.

CFA Exam Topic Area Weights

Topic Area	Level I	Level II	Level III
Ethical and Professional Standards (% of total)	*15*	*10*	*10*
Investment Tools	*50*	*30-60*	*0*
Corporate Finance	8	5-15	0
Economics*	10	5-10	0
Financial Reporting and Analysis	20	15-25	0
Quantitative Methods	12	5-10	0
Asset Classes	*30*	*35-75*	*35-45*
Alternative Investments	3	5-15	5-15
Derivatives	5	5-15	5-15
Equity Investments	10	20-30	5-15
Fixed Income	12	5-15	10-20
Portfolio Management and Wealth Planning	*5*	*5-15*	*45-55*
Total (%)	*100*	*100*	*100*

*Economics is part of Portfolio Management at Level III.
Source: CFA Institute, 2013-2014.

Some study sessions are quite long; schedule two weeks for these. Others are shorter; schedule four days. Most require one week. After you get going, you'll gain a better feel for how much time you need with the study sessions. Adjust the schedule as needed while making sure to cover each session adequately. No matter what, don't jeopardize the vital 45-day review date. Mind the critical path. (I provide sample week-by-week study schedules for Levels I, II, and III near the end of this book.)

Generally, 14 weeks is a prudent length of time for your first study period. However, this number isn't firm. If you have life events happening over these months, give yourself 16 weeks. If you're a speed reader or have tons of free time, shorten to 12 weeks. Though, you shouldn't move outside this range of 12 to 16 weeks.

While you contemplate this time period, plan a vacation! Seriously. Plan a vacation during March or April, if at all feasible. A long weekend, no more than a few days, away from the material and your study environment is good for your brain, your relationships, and your dedication to the CFA Program. If it makes you nervous to plan a break, begin your study agenda one week earlier. Having a vacation is more important than adhering to the 14-week timetable, though I scheduled 14 weeks for my first study period and still had time for a few days off. Each year, I planned a vacation in late March and did my best to leave the curriculum alone during those blissful days. I admit to bringing flashcards on my vacation at Levels II and III. If you are behind schedule or anxious about your preparation, consider doing the same. The vacation can still be regenerative, even if you lightly view study materials.

For the purposes of this hypothetical example, I'll assume you choose 14 weeks for your first critical-path phase. Recall that you are looking at April 23rd to start your second review of the material. Backing up 14 weeks lands you on January 15th. Tweak that date if you'd rather start on a Monday instead of the middle of a week. Now, you're ready to go.

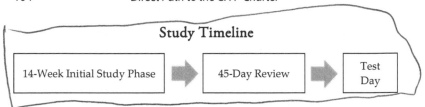

I suggest beginning in mid-January and taking the test in June. You know your critical-path tasks: a 14-week (three-and-a-half month) study phase followed by a 45-day review period. These two phases must not delay past their deadlines. Should you start falling behind, you must kick your studying into high gear. Finish these critical-path steps on time.

"Why not start the whole thing earlier?" the ambitious reader may ask. "For the June test, what's wrong with a start date in October or November? More study time certainly must be better than less, right?"

More study time isn't necessarily a bad thing. However, I'm assuming the reader wishes to accomplish two objectives during his or her CFA-testing experience: pass with a comfortable margin and escape the process with your life intact. If you devote 15 to 20 hours per week beginning in January, there's no need to start any earlier. The CFA curriculum only has to claim half of your year, not the entire twelve months.

The reader may ask, "What if I only want to study 10 hours per week instead of 15? Should I start earlier?"

I advise against it. Achieving a CFA designation is a grueling slog. Unless you have a seriously time-demanding job (and, if this is the case, passing the CFA Program may be a stretch for you), studying for five months instead of eight is worth the trade of working a little harder.

You'll already be studying most days beginning in January; study an extra half-hour. It's a small difference that means months—months!—of living in non-CFA studying bliss. Think very hard before you trade away that free time. Plus, this guards against the possibility of forgetting the material because you started too early, which is a very real danger. This is a big reason why I recommend beginning in January; you want your studying to occur close enough to test day that you remember it.

Additionally, studying during the November and December holidays is a bummer—and an unnecessary one for June candidates. Everyone deserves to enjoy their holidays without career stress, including CFA candidates. Take this time to let your mind rest and solidify relationships that become strained by June. Spend time with friends and family, do as much "nothing" as possible, and try not to think about January.

December candidates have other holidays around which they must schedule that can't be avoided. Do what you can to enjoy your holidays while not sacrificing the critical path.

If you are considering beginning with only four months to test day (February for the June test or August for the December test), stop. This is too late. Such a schedule only allows 10 weeks before the necessary 45-day final review. That isn't enough time for your first pass of the curriculum.

The 14-week schedule already proposes a start date in January, which won't allow for one week per study session. Some sessions are quite small and won't require a full week. This allows for a January start date, but not February.

Alright, your chosen day in January has rolled around. You have a documented study plan that will ensure you finish the first pass of material with 45 days to spare. You are ready to commence studying.

A Week in the Life of a CFA Candidate

From week to week, schedule the CFA Program around your life as much as possible rather than rearranging your life around the CFA Program. In the next few paragraphs, I lay out a general approach to organizing the weeks' study hours. You can also refer to the sample week-by-week plans and strategy pointers at the end of this book. However, these are only suggestions; your circumstances could demand a different schedule.

As the next few paragraphs describe the weekly time commitment and activities in each Level, refer to this chart, which provides a guideline for scheduling your study time:

Study Timeline with Weekly Hours

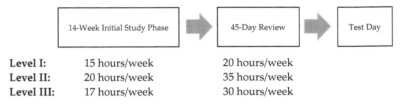

Level I:	15 hours/week	20 hours/week
Level II:	20 hours/week	35 hours/week
Level III:	17 hours/week	30 hours/week

For Level I's initial 14-week study phase, I suggest that you study approximately 15 hours per week, making sure to cover at least one study session each week and, sometimes, two. These 15 hours will include reading study notes, making flash cards, completing practice questions, reviewing the flashcards you just made, and anything else necessary to fully examine the subject.

In fitting these hours into your life, you might divide your week into a workweek and a weekend, and schedule with both in mind. Personally, I cherished my weekends and scheduled more studying within my workweek whenever possible. On a weekly basis, I studied Monday through Friday for 90 minutes between arriving home from work and dinner time. Luckily, my supportive significant other was willing to prepare most of my dinner meals, but a microwave also comes in handy. Additionally, I stole study minutes here and there during the workday while eating lunch, waiting in lines, riding public transportation, etc. Together, studying at work and home resulted in approximately 10 hours finished by the weekend. In the schedule I present in this chapter for Level I, you would have five hours remaining for the weekend.

As I previously mentioned, I studied too much in Level I, so I studied more like ten to fifteen hours over the weekends. You can aim for five. With this many hours, you can also allow yourself some flexibility. Perhaps you want to spend Saturday having lunch with a friend and catching a movie? Then all five hours of studying may occur on Sunday. Or, perhaps you decide to study two hours on Saturday and three on Sunday. Similarly, you might have religious commitments, family obligations, a social life, etc. Schedule around these occasions but don't let studying scheduled for the weekend be pushed into Monday. Falling behind is a slippery slope.

In Level II, 15 hours per week isn't enough during this initial study phase. I suggest you increase to 20 hours. Your weekly timetable also needs to become stricter. Be sure to have ten hours of studying accomplished by Friday. Then, plan for ten hours of studying over Saturday and Sunday, which is an estimate that may vary depending on the difficulty of the week's lessons.

Level III's weekly demands fell between those for Level I and II. I studied 10 hours during the work week and seven hours over the weekend during my initial study phase, which let me have a day off on occasion.

For all three Levels, when the 45-day second review period arrives, candidates' study time takes on a sense of urgency. Give the curriculum all the focus you can. Amplify your effort to 25 hours per week in Level I, 35 (or more) in Level II, and 30 in Level III. It's a great deal of studying, but it's necessary. You must cover everything a second time and take practice tests close enough to test day that you remember the specifics. That's why the 45-day review period isn't 60 days, 90 days, or longer. Because of the short 45-day timeframe, almost every waking hour outside of work or school must be devoted to studying. This is a strenuous period, but six weeks is bearable.

Don't Get Too Carried Away with Planning

Though it might appear otherwise, I didn't plan each and every day as closely as it may seem throughout my CFA-studying months. Candidates find that exact day-by-day plans need to be rewritten, so don't go to the trouble. Plan the 45-day review period precisely. But prior to then, planning each and every day is a fruitless activity since you can't know exactly how much time each page of the material will require. The goal is to create an outline that will put a fire under your rear if you start to lag behind schedule.

Above all, don't endanger the two critical-path deadlines. If necessary, adjust your weekly study hours as you go to make sure that you hit those due dates.

Your study plan is coming together. The next few chapters details what you'll be doing during these hundreds of hours and the strategies that can help you pass.

Key Takeaways: A Study Plan from Start to Finish

- Manage the CFA Program as a project with critical-path steps that must be completed on time and with sufficient quality. The two crucial segments are a 14-week initial study phase followed by a strict 45-day review period.

- Choose your Level I test date carefully. The Level I test can be taken in June or December, but taking the December exam may jeopardize your Level II performance if you aren't careful to make a solid plan for passing these exams back-to-back.

- Schedule your project's two critical phases by starting from your chosen test date. Move back 45 days to schedule the review period, and another 12 to 16 weeks to schedule the date to begin your initial study period. Now, you have start dates for your critical-path steps.

- During your first study phase, for Level I, you might study roughly 10 hours during the work week and another five over the weekend for a total of 15 each week. In Level II, study 20 hours per week during this initial study phase, and 17 per week in Level III.

- Increase your study hours during your final 45-day review period to 25 hours in Level I, 35 in Level II, and 30 in Level III. With this approach, the second review is packed as close to test day as possible so you'll remember the curriculum when it matters.

- Do whatever is necessary to meet your critical-path deadlines. Adjust your weekly study hours so that the two crucial phases begin and end on time.

CHAPTER 9

Curriculum Books or Study Notes?

The CFA curriculum books are lengthy, and that doesn't mean only the page count. Besides the sheer number of pages (thousands), the individual paragraphs, examples, and practice problems can go on and on and *on*.

The pages are crowded and very slow reads. Superfluous information turns what could be a quick practice question into a full-page epic about Bob and Mary who met in college, read spy novels, and enjoy fishing (who cares). Likewise, the authors sprinkle historical perspective throughout the text that, while interesting, wastes time. When you *finally* turn the current page to the next, you are greeted by more drawn-out prose. The curriculum feels never-ending.

There's one common dilemma that you and every other candidate confront in the CFA Program: "Must I read these tedious curriculum books? Or can I just buy a good set of study materials and call it a day?"

Candidates must find a way to adequately cover the material without sacrificing their day jobs. Many turn to third-party study notes for help.

For each Level, a handful of companies provide A-to-Z study programs containing study notes, practice questions, practice tests, flashcards, video lectures, etc. Study notes are the heart of each company's offering. These are better described as summaries which reduce each curriculum book by at least half. While the study notes can't be described as brief, they substantially trim the curriculum.

Can study notes completely replace the curriculum? Candidates want that to be the case, if merely to carry around lighter books. The answer depends on which Level you are attempting.

Curriculum Books Not Necessary in Level I

Rarely does anyone cite Level I as the most difficult Level (this title typically goes to Level II), yet the scale of the Level I syllabus often results in candidates labeling it as the second hardest.

The Level I curriculum textbooks are the bulkiest. I have met only two people who read the Level I curriculum books in their entirety. For everyone else—including me—they were too much. I suggest skimming the books, if you read them at all.

Though perhaps not great for reading, curriculum books can be useful for other purposes. Mainly, they contain decent practice questions at the end of every chapter with valuable explanations. The questions and explanations are sometimes longwinded, but many CFA charterholders credit these end-of-reading exercises for helping them pass. I relied more on third-party practice questions, but if I had to do it again, I would use both.

Additionally, most of the curriculum books' Ethics session should be read—actually, *pored over*—multiple times. As a reminder, you can skip the Ethics cases.

All in all, don't toss the curriculum books aside, though consider alternatives for the long texts.

In Level I, third-party study notes can almost fully replace the CFA Institute's curriculum book readings. Because the Level I subject matter isn't extremely challenging, study notes tend to cover the full curriculum in adequate detail. Except for the Ethics study session, I never opened a Level I curriculum book. I relied exclusively on third-party study notes to learn every concept and scored in the highest percentile in every testing category without reading a single word of the curriculum.

The CFA Institute prefers, understandably, that candidates use the curriculum books. More importantly, I trust the CFA Institute wants candidates to know the information contained in the books, regardless how that knowledge was acquired.

The CFA Institute takes an interesting approach in encouraging use of the curriculum books. I often refer to test prep providers as "third parties," but many have monetary affiliations with the CFA Institute. The CFA Institute runs a Prep Provider Guidelines Program that collects money from test preparation services in exchange for benefits such as advertising on the CFA Institute's website and in exam centers.[20] As you consider test prep services, remember that when a provider appears in CFA Institute publications as a featured service, the provider paid for that advertising through an annual fee.

To be allowed into this lucrative program, providers must give disclaimers affirming that study notes should not be used as a replacement for the curriculum in any CFA Level. In its program manual, the CFA Institute states that providers must, "Endorse the value and importance of the CFA Institute curriculum in effectively preparing for the exams and ... convey that provider products should be used as supplementary tools, and not as a replacement for the curriculum." Providers have a huge incentive to participate; by having this disclaimer and paying a fee, they get access to your mailing address, test results (in aggregate with other candidates using its service), and other information. This is how marketing materials for third-party study systems mysteriously show up in your mailbox throughout the CFA Program; the CFA Institute sold your mailing address. I didn't know it until after I finished the CFA Program, but you can opt out by changing your preferences in your online CFA Institute account. The CFA Institute's privacy policy is easily accessible; most candidates don't know to read it, but I wish I had.

All in all, as you consider test preparation services, be skeptical of providers' statements suggesting how you should or should not use study notes; there is money behind these disclaimers. I don't fault either side for taking part in these transactions. You simply need to know what's going on behind the scenes.

For me, the Level I curriculum books were generally unnecessary. Unless you have extra time and relish the opportunity to read tremendous amounts of heavy information, choose the least painful path to a passing score.

However, if you decide to ditch the curriculum, here are a few words of caution. Skip nothing in the third party materials. Nothing. The study notes are condensed versions of the full curriculum, so only critical information makes it into the third-party resources. Therefore, you must read them thoroughly if you plan to ignore the curriculum books. No skimming or skipping. Read every word and example.

As long as you use third-party study notes properly, the Level I curriculum books can serve as reinforcing material. Solve the curriculum books' practice questions and befriend the Ethics sections, but consider letting study notes teach the concepts.

Give the Level II and III Curriculum Books More Attention

Skip ahead to when you have passed Level I and are preparing for Level II. You might decide to use the same strategy and again avoid the curriculum books. Don't make this common mistake. I get it—changing your study approach between Levels is difficult. You were successful at Level I using only third-party materials. Why mess with success? It is a natural human tendency to resist change, and I made the same mistake. I didn't crack the spine on a single CFA Institute book until Level III. I approached Level II using the same strategy that I followed at Level I because it was such a success. But Level II is a whole new ballgame. Third-party study systems simply cannot compete with the curriculum in terms of preparing you to pass these higher Levels.

Even after studying 600 hours, third-party materials didn't prepare me as well for the Level II exam as I should have been with so much effort expended. Walking out of the testing room, I was sure that I had failed. When my Level II test results arrived, I was shocked to see a passing score. For a while, I was convinced the CFA Institute accidentally sent me someone else's results.

The study notes did me few time-saving favors. I spent many hours deciphering concepts in my study materials that were oversimplified to the point of confusing the reader. As I completed practice questions, I continually found gaps in my understanding that I had to address by returning to concepts that I already covered. Through my Level III experience, I found out that I would have saved time by following the concepts in the curriculum books instead. Utilizing the curriculum would have shaved hours off my study regimen and secured a more comfortable passing margin. Better results with less time is preferable to struggling through third-party materials almost as long and complex as the real thing.

Some adaptability would have served me well. I became comfortable with my study program and I didn't want to acclimate to the increased demands of Level II. This was stupid, and I nearly paid a year of extra studying for my stupidity. Don't repeat my mistake. If a certain strategy is not working, give it a couple more weeks to see if you can work out the kinks. If not, scrap it. To determine if a strategy is working or not, do practice problems every week; you should ace your recently reviewed subjects. If even the subject you reviewed a few days ago is giving you trouble, consider a new strategy.

After my close call, I learned my lesson. At Level III, I used the curriculum extensively in conjunction with my third-party materials. I spent more time with the curriculum readings, while my study notes helped explain complicated parts and illustrated concepts with additional examples. Level III is a difficult test, but using curriculum readings and third-party study notes along with my other critical tools like flashcards, practice questions, and practice tests made me a confident, ready Level III candidate.

In Levels II and III, the curriculum books should be your primary study tool. When your books arrive for these Levels, make an appointment with your chiropractor. You'll need to see him or her in a few weeks when your back cramps from carrying these bricks—I mean books—everywhere you go. The curriculum weighs about 20 pounds. With your test registration fee, you've purchased books that double as very expensive exercise weights. How convenient, since you will no longer have time for the gym!

The curriculum books are so vital at the higher Levels that you could refrain from buying study notes at all. The curriculum books—not study notes—are the more essential aids in Levels II and III. Third-party materials are still useful, though. If you can afford it, the extra resources can help clarify tough subjects and provide further examples.

Level I is the only Level that can be conquered without the curriculum books. The Level II and III exams cover more complicated concepts that can't be summarized well without losing necessary information. Though, overall, third-party materials were a key component of my study regimen at every Level and should be considered for yours.

Mandatory Study Note Qualities

Study notes should have certain characteristics which, thankfully, most of the available third-party study notes have. At a minimum, the notes should cover every study session from the curriculum, be heavily oriented towards examples, and avoid oversimplifying concepts for the sake of getting you through the material as quickly as possible. The major risk with study notes is that too much summarization eliminates obscure but testable concepts; watch out for this risk.

CFA-test questions often contain twists, nuances, and traps, and your study notes should prepare you for these obstacles. In the curriculum, each problem is paired with a solution sequence that will find the correct answer most of the time. But, there are always exceptions. The CFA Institute frequently tests candidates on the exceptions; it's a great way to determine which candidates are the most proficient. A good set of study notes will explain both the standard approach to a concept and the myriad ways in which the CFA Institute may complicate the issue on test day. Bad study notes will only give a "most of the time" solution and leave you blissfully unaware of the important information you're missing until your test results arrive.

I will cover flashcards thoroughly in the next chapter, but a quick word about flashcards in relation to study notes: Creating flashcards from your study notes should be a simple task as key concepts, definitions, and equations almost jump off the page and yell, "I am flashcard material!" Such critical items are typically offset in bold or highlighted font drawing your attention to the most important matters. If everything looks equally important—in other words, you can't discern the most significant slices of information that should become flashcards—check the return date on your study material. Send it back and order from another vendor.

The Endless Debate: Which Study Notes Are Best?

(A friendly reminder: I have no affiliation with, or endorsement from, any of the companies mentioned in this book. Further, the opinions I put forth about both the CFA Institute and third-party service providers are only that—my opinions.)

There are many quality providers of CFA course materials. Candidates might consider Kaplan Schweser, Elan Guides, AnalystNotes, and Allen Resources, just to name some well-known companies. (Check out the more comprehensive list in the "Test Preparation Resources" section, including brief descriptions of the features and costs of each one.)

Take a look at online discussion boards regarding the CFA Program. There is an ongoing near frenzy over this eternal question: Which third-party study notes are the best? When forking over a sizable chunk of money for study materials, all candidates are concerned with making the best choice, and rightfully so.

Obviously, you want to choose notes that will help achieve a passing score. However, there isn't one perfect study notes option. I realize this may sound like a copout, but all of the third-party providers create their systems from the same six books—the CFA curriculum. We spend countless hours debating between fairly similar alternatives.

Most third-party providers charge roughly $1,000 at each Level for a full study system that includes study notes. Study notes can be purchased separately from the complete system, but practice questions, mock exams, and other perks like video lectures may be worth the extra cost of the package deal.

Some study systems cost less. I started Level I with two sets of materials: the Schweser program costing approximately $1,000 (that I luckily borrowed from a friend) and a subscription to AnalystNotes.com for $99. In the second week, I abandoned my Schweser materials and relied solely on AnalystNotes for most of my Level I study needs. Schweser was not a bad program and many candidates pass using Schweser materials. However, the Schweser study notes were laid out in a manner that didn't suit me and the initial chapters appeared to include more summary rather than more detail. I preferred less summarization and turned elsewhere.

By avoiding expensive systems, I saved money and still passed Level I with handsome scores. AnalystNotes was my lifesaver with exhaustive study notes, practice questions, review quizzes, and practice exams. Its resources are online; AnalystNotes will not mail you booklets of study notes and practice questions like Schweser will. However, the website approach allows subscribers to post comments throughout the notes, providing additional learning opportunities as users ask questions and get answers online from each other. I was able to print these notes, as well, and take the user discussions with me. Many other test prep providers are also exclusively online; I am told that most offer a printing benefit as a great option for days when you can't be in front of a computer. This helps relieve the need for physical booklets.

Unfortunately, after Level I, my study notes experience wasn't so carefree. For Level II, I again used AnalystNotes but, at this higher Level, I experienced trouble with gaps and unclear explanations. In talking with candidates, I've heard that many experience similar issues in Level II using other vendors' study notes as well. This suggests that overreliance on study notes in general can be a problem in Levels II and III rather than specific vendors. I believe my difficulties were largely due to the fact that I was relying solely on study notes and not using the curriculum. I still passed, so the notes were sufficient with enough study hours. If I had to study for Level II again, though, I would consider trying a different vendor rather than AnalystNotes. Variety is a good thing in the CFA Program because it gives you new perspectives and keeps you sharp and attentive. However, I would still use the AnalystNotes practice questions, practice tests, and quizzes in Level II, which were again very useful as they were in Level I.

For Level III, I used study notes, but not extensively. AnalystNotes does not provide Level III study materials, so I switched to Schweser. With the Schweser study notes, I encountered problems like the ones I had with my AnalystNotes guides the year before. This was further evidence for me that Levels II and III are better suited to using the curriculum books with study notes as a supplement. I expected this, so I used Schweser study notes sparingly in comparison to my use of the curriculum book readings.

For any Level, newer course providers may be worth checking out as they might provide lower prices while still meeting the general requirements of a study program. Almost all providers offer a return policy, so pick a program and try it out.

When shopping for your study notes, keep in mind the minimum standards for all study notes. They must be comprehensive, understandable, and easily convertible to flashcards. I would assert that most third-party providers meet these standards. Candidates who fail the CFA tests tend to do so because they abuse the study notes concept rather than any study notes deserving the blame.

Study notes alone are not the path to a passing result. If that were the case, a large majority would pass since a large majority uses third-party study notes. The notes serve one function and one function only: distill the curriculum into a practical size. You still must do just as many practice questions, create just as many flashcards, and take just as many practice tests.

All study notes have their limits. Take a look at the money-back guarantee on your potential study system. If you fail the CFA exam, most third-party suppliers will refund your money. But, the guarantee comes with fine print stating that your money will be given back only if you answer at least 90 percent of all practice questions on the provider's website correctly (the percentage hurdle varies). There are generally thousands of questions that must be answered with a nearly unattainable success rate. Vendors know that the notes alone won't carry you through to a passing score. Reading the study notes doesn't create a working knowledge of the curriculum—practice questions do. If you are performing well on practice questions, it's unlikely that you will fail the test. Vendors prefer no refunds, so they connect the money-back guarantee to a more reliable gauge of your preparation.

The quality of your study notes matters but is not the key to a passing score. Weak study notes are problematic, particularly if you replace the curriculum with study notes in Level I. However, weak study notes are not the industry standard. If you are concerned about the quality of your study notes, use both the CFA Institute curriculum and your notes for a few weeks. Both should impart an equivalent understanding of the concepts. Once you feel comfortable with your study notes, rely on them more heavily. Remember, in Levels II and III, study notes are a clarifying tool rather than a replacement of the curriculum.

Apply Brainpower to More Pressing Issues

Overall, the debate about which study notes to buy is less critical than you might imagine. Every third-party study program produces passing candidates and failing candidates, again implying that study notes may not be the reason for failing scores.

The CFA Program usually defeats candidates due to weak time management or poor preparation practices, not the choice of study notes. Assess the study note landscape, pick one, and move forward to more critical aspects of your study plan.

Key Takeaways: Curriculum Books or Study Notes?

- Third-party companies offer CFA study materials for each Level, which generally include study notes, example problems, practice questions, flashcards, and practice tests.

- Candidates debate about which study notes are best, but those who fail the tests tend to do so because they abuse the study notes concept. Study notes are not the key to passing. Practice questions, flashcards, and other study aids make a bigger difference.

- Most third-party study notes meet the mandatory standards: cover every study session, include many example problems, avoid oversimplifying the curriculum, and convert to flashcards. If your study notes do not have these qualities, return them and choose a different vendor.

- Though you might prefer study notes for reading material, the curriculum books are still useful in every Level. Complete the curriculum practice questions, and read the Ethics sessions numerous times before test day.

- In Level I, study notes can fully replace the CFA Institute curriculum writings (I relied on AnalystNotes). However, this only works if you're willing to slowly and thoroughly review every word of those notes. Additionally, the other study aids become even more essential.

- In Levels II and III, the study notes cannot replace the curriculum books. There is little that can be substantially summarized or simplified. Instead, the curriculum books should serve as your main study medium, while third-party notes help you focus on key points.

CHAPTER 10

The Power of Flashcards

Flashcards are boring. They are no fun to make and even less fun to review. I hate flashcards. However, I owe my CFA success to flashcards. Flashcards are the reason that I passed. Not study notes, not the curriculum, not even practice tests. Flashcards.

What is a flashcard? At its most basic, a flashcard is a small piece of paper that states a term or name of an equation on one side and the definition of that term or mathematical equation on the other. Often in the CFA Program, a concept may fall into both categories. For example, "free cash flow" is both a term and the name of an equation that could appear on the front of a flashcard, and you would write the definition and the equation on the back.

Lists are also good candidates for flashcards. The CFA Institute loves lists; these are scattered throughout the study sessions. You'll find theories, too. With so many terms, equations, concepts, theories, and lists to remember, you'll soon be drowning in flashcards. To review them is simple: Read whatever is written on the front of the flashcard and try to remember whatever is on the back.

The Merits of Flashcards as a Study Tool

Flashcards are monotonous and painful to study. But, they have merits that no other study medium can equal. In your CFA-test preparation toolbox, flashcards serve as the hammer that pounds concepts into your brain. Even if you had the opportunity to review the curriculum multiple times before test day, there is too much information to fit into your head without distilling it into a quick, reviewable form. More essentially, flashcards force you to think about each concept before flipping the cards to see the answer. Study notes are also reviewable but, with the answers right there on the same page, you might as well be reading a novel at the beach.

Flashcards condense the curriculum into short, manageable nuggets while stimulating your brain to convert the concepts to long term memory. Each Level contains massive amounts of material and simply reading pages and pages of text isn't going to cut it.

I had a very naïve response when my curriculum books arrived for Level I: "This isn't so bad! I can memorize 2,000 pages in six months, no problem!" Yeah, right. The CFA Institute doesn't want you to just memorize it; you must deeply understand the concepts. It is very possible that the test includes an off-the-wall financial model only mentioned in a single paragraph on page 541 of the 4th book. During my Level III test, one question was so obscure that I literally laughed out loud.

Though you could be tested on any concept, you can't put every word of the curriculum into flashcard form. That's not the point of flashcards. Instead, people who pass the CFA tests *know* the regular material, which gives them time to work out the correct answers to the random questions. You must master the non-obscure concepts. This is where flashcards come to the rescue.

Knowledgeable candidates can fail the CFA tests simply because they can't bring information to the forefront of their memories quickly enough on test day. Most candidates who fail these tests know the material, but the answers are buried under the twelve thousand other things they learned in the previous six months. Flashcards can help solve this problem. They help you overcome test day nerves and regurgitate information studied weeks ago. Flashcards turn you into a CFA-test taking machine spitting out correct answers like a genius in a children's trivia match.

This brings me to the most valuable advantage of flashcards: Flashcards are portable. Their portability allows you to study anywhere.

During my studying years, I reviewed flashcards all day long. My lunch breaks at work revolved around flashcards. I reviewed flashcards in line at the grocery store. I'd review a few more during my daily exercise routine. I spent many hours reviewing flashcards on my long commute to and from work. I reviewed flashcards while I got ready in the morning, and then before bed at night. Flashcards dominated my life, particularly during the 45-day review period before each test. It was miserable. But, without a doubt, flashcards are the reason I passed.

How to Use Flashcards to Their Full Potential

Begin your flashcard regimen by working through a study session and either creating your own flashcards as you go or referring to a purchased set. Some major test prep vendors offer flashcards, so you can get away with not creating many. However, expect these third-party flashcards to be expensive, high-level in substance, and only available in digital form. Due to these drawbacks, I always made my own flashcards and avoided the third-party options. If you decide to buy a set, supplement the inevitable holes by making additional flashcards as necessary to ensure that every equation and concept is covered.

Whether purchased or self-created, number your flashcards both in numerical order and to match the study session. For example, the cards for session 14 should be labeled 14-1, 14-2, 14-3, and so on. This is an important step because concepts in study sessions tend to build on each other. When you are first reviewing flashcards, studying them in order will yield better memorization results than a random, jumbled approach. Later, mix up the cards (within each study session) to make sure you can remember that topic's concepts without a precursor flashcard.

There is nothing more frustrating than dropping your flashcards and mixing study sessions together. Remember, topics on the exams are kept separate from each other, so keep each topic's flashcards separate from other topics. I remember cursing the rock I tripped on at Level I, sending my unnumbered flashcards flying everywhere. You'll be glad you took the time to number them.

As you near the end of each study session and finish making its related flashcards, immediately review that session's flashcards once. Then set them aside and move to the next study session. After reading through the next study session and creating yet another pile of flashcards, immediately review that session's flashcards once, and move to the next study session.

To illustrate, consider study session 12. Read the session 12 material, do practice problems, and make flashcards as you go. When you feel as if session 12 has been adequately covered, review the session 12 flashcards once. Now, move to session 13 and repeat the same process.

Continue through the curriculum in this fashion, completing your first pass of the material in its entirety 45 days prior to the test date. Immediately reviewing each session's flashcards helps reinforce everything learned within that session without consuming too much time. Don't review any prior session's flashcards during this time; there will be a 45 day review period for that.

By the end of the flashcard-making process, you should have a sizable pile of cards. At Level I, you should finish with about 300 flashcards in total. This may sound like a bit much, but consider that 300 flashcards works out to only about 17 flashcards per study session. Considering how expansive the study sessions can be, this is a limited number. Try not to think about Level II, where 600 flashcards await. Level III yields approximately 450 flashcards.

Reviewing Flashcards during the Second Review Phase

In your final 45-day review period, you'll go back to study the hundreds of flashcards you spent the last few months creating. At Level I, if you review only 25 flashcards per day, you'll finish reviewing all 300 flashcards in less than two weeks.

However, I don't suggest reviewing all of your flashcards straight through from beginning to end within the first two weeks of your 45-day review period. Instead, review each study session independently over a few days. Spend time doing a number of practice problems for one study session and review your notes. Then, review the flashcards for that session *twice* in immediate succession before moving on to the next session. Set aside any flashcards still giving you trouble; you will drill these in the last week before the moment of reckoning.

Taking session 8 as an example, begin by reading session 8's study notes and key areas of the curriculum while making flashcards. Complete practice problems. Then, go through all of session 8's flashcards twice before moving to session 9. Be sure to segregate session 8 flashcards that give you trouble for later review.

As you study the flashcards, think about each one. Don't cheat by turning over each card immediately without critically thinking about the concept. Also, during the 45-day review period, make sure to work through each session's flashcards twice. This double-pass approach will quicken your testing speed and help you remember more information. You'll be surprised at how much you can retain in those last 45 days.

Flashcards work. If you don't believe me, try them. Study one session with flashcards and one without to see which one you remember a week later. Even an hour later. I have not met a single CFA charterholder who regrets using flashcards. In fact, I meet very few CFA charterholders who didn't use flashcards, but I've met plenty of failing candidates who skipped them. So, please, include flashcards as a supporting tool in your study endeavors. Certainly do not replace your study notes or the curriculum, but let the flashcards be the hammer that drives the information into your memory.

Key Takeaways: The Power of Flashcards

- Use flashcards to drive the most important pieces of the CFA curriculum into your long-term memory. The CFA curriculum contains hundreds of terms, equations, concepts, theories, and lists that you must remember quickly and confidently.

- Create your own flashcards or buy them online. If you buy flashcards, watch out for holes in the third-party set. Produce your own individual flashcards where the purchased set falls short.

- Make flashcards during your first pass of the curriculum from January through mid-April (or July through mid-October if you are taking the Level I test in December). Generate flashcards as you work through each study session.

- Number the cards in order and note the study session for each one. For example, the cards for session 14 should be labeled 14-1, 14-2, 14-3, and so on.

- Conclude each study session by reviewing that session's flashcards once before moving on to the next session. Be sure to finish this complete process at least 45 days before the test.

- Finish with approximately 300 flashcards in total at Level I, 600 at Level II, and 450 at Level III. These are approximations; dependent on the amount of information per card, the count could be less or more.

- Review all of your flashcards in the final 45-day period together with your other study materials. During this second pass at the curriculum, study one topic or session at a time. For each subject, review the curriculum, your notes, and practice problems over a few days. Then, drill that topic's flashcards twice in succession.

- Set aside any flashcards still giving you trouble as you continue through the study sessions. Review the "problem" flashcards again in the last week before the test.

- Challenge yourself to think about each card. Flashcards are basically miniature practice problems. Don't read the front and then immediately turn it over to find the answer. By critically considering each flashcard, you'll commit that information to long term memory.

CHAPTER 11

Transforming Knowledge into Test Performance

We start the CFA Program to learn and, indeed, you will. Candidates seldom trip up on the learning part of the CFA Program. It's the testing that causes problems.

Bluntly put, you need to pass the tests. Sure, sure ... learn, too. But the CFA Program isn't a celebration of the beautiful profession of finance. It is a series of tests. It doesn't spend a week evaluating your on-the-job expertise. It doesn't ask your IQ, or request a 50-page paper on why you should be granted a CFA charter. Simply "learning" only gets you part way there.

Instead, the Program evaluates your ability to answer financial questions correctly given three possible answers, plus essay questions at Level III. So, practice! A lot! If you want to pass CFA tests, practice passing CFA tests.

Before going further, let me debunk the idea that focusing on a "pass" at Level I will impact your performance at Level II, and so on. Ideally you'd focus less on the grade and more on absorbing the subject matter. Unfortunately, CFA exams are only given once or twice a year, eliminating much hope of that. The consequences are too high. You need a passing score.

The inherent structure of the CFA Program encourages candidates to focus on their scores above all else. The CFA Institute tries to mitigate this tendency through the multi-level structure of the Program. In school, you took Algebra I and then Algebra II, suggesting the second class built on the first. However, as a student, that wasn't necessarily my experience. The advanced class didn't build on the last so much as take my studies in a new direction. Similarly, at no point in the CFA Program did I think, "I wish I learned that concept more completely last year." Instead, the Levels teach new perspectives, theories, and equations, while repeating any necessary information from the Level before to ensure that the candidate fully understands the session. If you managed to pass last year, you studied enough to remember the basics for this year. The Level's curriculum fills in the rest.

I came away from the CFA Program with a conceptual knowledge of every financial subject under the sun. This definitely helps in my day-to-day work because I have a broader understanding of the financial world. But I admit some specifics are fuzzy because I studied to pass. I learned about the topic, but I spent more time learning how to answer questions on it. This isn't necessarily a bad thing—I still own the curriculum books, which serve as great reference material. Plus, the Internet knows everything.

Practice Passing CFA Exams

I took practice tests in studying for each Level, and you should, too, whether you generally test well or not. I'm naturally good at taking tests (luckily), as you may be. In the CFA Program, this doesn't eradicate the need for practice tests. Practice tests gauge your ongoing performance, reduce test day anxiety, and reveal the tricky stuff. Even if you're not nervous at all, you need to gauge where you stand. Moreover, why attempt an endeavor this important without ample practice?

Few pop culture examples portray a better argument for practicing than television shows that showcase cooking competitions. These shows generally follow the same pattern; chefs are challenged to design, prepare, and cook a dish within a specified timeframe using a soon-to-be announced secret ingredient. Whoever cooks the worst dish will be kicked off the show.

"Chefs, please cook a restaurant-quality dish with chicken as the main ingredient. You have 30 minutes, and your time starts now." The chefs run off to the pantry to collect ingredients and rush back to their cooking stations. The chef breathlessly explain their dishes as they begin boiling water, cutting vegetables, and heating stoves. At this point, I am frequently shouting at the television because, too often, a chef starts the description of his or her dish by announcing, "I've never made this dish before, but ..." *What?!* Your life revolves around cooking. You've cooked thousands of dishes, and you defeated hundreds of other chefs who vied for your spot on this television show. Yet you are choosing to make a dish that you have never once practiced? It's chicken for goodness' sake! Surely, you've made a dish with chicken before—make that!

Many times, this is the chef who is bid farewell as the other chefs chose to make dishes they *have* practiced. When other competitors practice, you stand little chance of finishing ahead if you do not. In the CFA Program, your fellow candidates will practice. Give yourself a chance to compete.

Developing a Practice Test Strategy

I recommend taking at least four practice tests (also known as mock exams) at each Level. Some candidates will take eight, some will take two, and some won't take any. With four, you're prepared without going over the top. (Remember, if you are not native to the English language, consider adding to this number and completing seven.) There are only so many ways that the test designers can confuse you on these exams; by the end of several practice tests, you'll notice the usual trickery.

Most practice tests integrate the tests' tactics as realistically as possible. The non-CFA Institute providers can't know what's going to be on the real test, yet they come surprisingly close. Plus, the answer sheets explain why the correct answers are correct, which is a learning tool in itself.

Don't jump into practice tests too early. Hold off until your final 45-day review period. There's little value in taking practice tests before this point as you haven't covered all of the subjects yet. Once this period begins (in other words, you've finished your first review of the material) then start taking practice tests.

There are six weeks during the 45-day review period. Spread the practice tests over these weeks, making sure you take one in the first week and one in the last. The regular repetition turns you into a test-taking bloodhound; you can smell the snares immediately and detecting them becomes second nature.

The mock exams not only help you to prepare for the intellectual material, but they'll also teach you the tests' logistics. For example, you'll discover that the test questions in Levels I and

II are grouped together by study sessions. For instance, a fixed income question is located with the other fixed income questions. You don't have to wonder, "Is this a fixed income question or wealth management?" You'll know, because the test paper says so. That's a huge help because the test mirrors the way you've studied—essentially, thinking about one topic at a time.

The logistics are more elaborate in Level III, which, again, calls for practice tests. The answer sheet looks different and is very picky about where you can and can't write your essay answers. Level III test prep providers know this creates a challenge for many candidates, so they try to emulate the CFA Institute's answer sheet. I know candidates who were completely confused during their Level III test because they hadn't practiced. They spent precious test time figuring out the answer sheet instead of the answers, ran out of time, and failed.

Practice tests are enormously helpful. I looked forward to my practice tests because they told me the truth about my testing readiness. View them as a personal challenge to do better on the next practice test than you did on the last.

In taking practice tests, you don't need to mimic the test day experience on every one. Constantly repeating the full six-hour hoopla wears you out. Definitely take one full test with a timed lunch to see what it's like. For the others, break each into two pieces.

The tests contain two sessions—morning and afternoon—that can be easily completed on different days. Simply take the "morning" session early in the week, and take the "afternoon" session over the weekend. This plan averts fatigue—constantly taking six-hour behemoth exams is exhausting. Three-hour tests are far more digestible into your regular study regimen (and your life). Practice often with these half tests, mimicking morning and afternoon sessions without claiming your entire Saturday. It also keeps you in a test-taking mindset by practicing often.

Your Practice Test Options

I took lots of practice tests at each Level, but finding them on a budget wasn't easy. All test preparation services provide practice exams, but they're generally not cheap. I began at AnalystNotes.com, which provided access to five quality, difficult practice tests for less than $100. (To repeat myself, I have no affiliation with this website.) That's an insanely good deal for tests that challenge you.

Also, if you are registered for a CFA exam, you already have access to one practice exam. The CFA Institute provides one complimentary mock exam with your registration, which you can complete on your home computer whenever it suites your study regimen. Strangely, for me, this practice test was the least similar to the real thing. I've heard other candidates say it was very helpful for them, so maybe mine was an anomaly. Either way, take the CFA Institute's practice test—just don't expect it to perfectly represent the actual test.

If neither of these options appeal to you, some online providers offer mock exams that are quite popular. In Levels II and III, even though I relied mostly on AnalystNotes for practice tests, I added a Schweser exam or two into the mix for another perspective. I sourced these additional tests from friends who had taken my Level the year before. The curriculum changes little from year to year, thus last year's practice test covers almost exactly the same material as this year's extremely expensive practice test. You can even look up on the CFA Institute's website exactly what changes were made to the curriculum since the last exam, which are usually limited to adding a couple readings and deleting a few others. Assuming that you practice enough, taking older practice tests is normally fine. And, if nothing else, extra practice tests offer a great supply of example problems. As a caveat, the CFA Institute can, at any time, radically change the test or the curriculum and using older practice tests carries a risk.

If you're looking for more practice exams, the CFA Institute provides some in the form of $40 sample tests. The sample tests are only two hours in length and therefore not a great value. However, you may want to consider them if you're having trouble finding additional practice tests or feel that you need extra training.

Once you've collected a sufficient number of practice exams, schedule them into a calendar. Take one when your 45-day review period begins to gauge your comprehension after months of studying. Take a couple more over the following weeks spacing the morning and afternoon sessions some days apart. Finally, reserve your last rehearsal for the weekend before test day. The results will guide your last few days of studying and prime you for your live performance.

If You Are Wrestling with the Material, Practice Tests Can Help!

Some topics in the CFA curriculum won't be your cup of tea. Ask any seasoned candidate which CFA subjects he or she dislikes, and you'll get a quick, lamenting response. We know what our challenges are.

Practice tests can help candidates grapple with their weaknesses. You might not shine in certain areas, but enough practice improves your performance to an acceptable level. It's amazing what practice can do.

Until I went off to college, my childhood waking hours were devoted to two activities: school and gymnastics. Few sports bow down to the gods of practice like gymnastics. Before school, after school, on weekends. Day in, day out, 365 days a year. There's no such thing as an off season. The longest vacation I took from the sport in over 10 years was a mere five days. Thankfully, my parents were not the crazy type—I could quit at any time. But I loved gymnastics like few others ever have.

Unfortunately, I didn't have a drop of gymnastics talent in my entire body. It was as if I'd gotten lost on my way to a track field. Adding to my misplacement in this sport, I attended an academy coached by former Olympians that boasted some of the nation's best young gymnasts. I preserved my spot on the team by practicing with unmatched intensity. It was amazing what I would overcome with a commitment to practice.

I began my gymnastics career as the worst vaulter in the world. Statistics aren't kept on such things, but my coaches and I were convinced. Seriously, it was a mess. Over and over, I'd sprint down the runway, crash into the vaulting table like a horrific car wreck, and fall in a puddle on the other side. I'd watch my talented teammates time their steps down the runway, jump on the springboard's sweet spot, and flip with effortlessly executed movements to a sound landing. And again, they'd watch me crash. I quickly came to hate the vault. But I had a coach who wouldn't give up on me. "You'll just have to practice harder than the others." And that's what I did.

Slowly, the crashes became controlled chaos. Months later, the controlled chaos became harnessed power, and I started placing in competitions. Four years later, I was the best vaulter in our accomplished gym. Soon, I was the best in the state. I felt more at home vaulting than walking. My vaulting reputation so drastically improved that my teammates forgot that I was ever a vaulting disaster. I'm told that my coaches still reminisce about that girl who made the miraculous vaulting turnaround. It wasn't a miracle. Rather than strike the skill from my gymnastics repertoire, I practiced. And now, more than anything else from my childhood gymnastics days, I miss the vault.

I feel the same way about the CFA Program. Parts of the curriculum felt like crashing into the vault. Practice tests highlighted my weak spot, which was the Finacial Reporting and Analysis topic. I'd had little exposure to accounting, and I disliked the competing international accounting rules versus American rules. Can't we all agree on one set of accounting rules?! I struggled. Soon, I realized, thanks to practice tests, that I would fail Level II if I didn't overhaul my study regimen and do far more financial statement practice questions. I did, and I passed. I still didn't outperform on that section, but I performed well enough to pass. Now I have a job that relies on financial statement analysis, and I like it.

Most importantly, practice tests turn months of learning into something you can act upon. In its entirety, before starting practice tests, the curriculum floated around in my head like one big cloud. I knew the information, but couldn't articulate it well. I hoped I understood the material instead of knowing that I did.

Practice tests can do wonders to both spotlight your weaknesses and help turn all of your knowledge into correct answers.

The Golden Rule

You might know the curriculum inside and out, but testing is a different mission. Again, remember the golden rule: you need to pass CFA tests, so practice passing CFA tests.

Everyone else will practice. You must to do better than average, so consider practicing more than an average candidate. I can't say how many practice tests the typical candidate takes, but it's more than zero.

Everyone learns the curriculum, but only a small percentage pass the exam. What sets some candidates apart is the ability to put that understanding on paper. Practice.

Key Takeaways: Transforming Knowledge into Test Performance

- Learn the curriculum, but also learn how to test on the curriculum. If you want to pass CFA tests, practice passing CFA tests.

- Prepare for the test's tempting wrong answers by exposing yourself to typical test questions. You might be great at taking tests but, the tests contain tricks for which you'll only be ready if you've practiced. Other candidates will practice, and you should as well.

- Use practice exams to help you overcome curriculum weaknesses and turn broad, abstract knowledge into correct answers on test day.

- Take at least four practice tests in preparing for each Level. If the English language might pose a challenge, consider taking seven or more. However, don't start practice tests until you've made it to your final 45-day review period. Then, spread them out over those final six weeks.

- Schedule one mock exam as a full, six-hour rehearsal that mimics a real test day experience. Otherwise, break the remaining practice tests into two pieces using the morning and afternoon sessions. Disperse the two sessions on different days to avoid testing fatigue.

- Evaluate the numerous practice test providers and determine which ones you'll use. In addition to your CFA Institute mock test, consider AnalystNotes for inexpensive Level I and Level II tests. Many candidates are successful using Schweser tests, although they cost more. Other providers also provide valuable practice tests.

- Rely on old practice tests at your own risk. Though the curriculum usually doesn't change much from year to year, the CFA Institute can surprise us. If you include older practice tests in your study regimen, employ some current ones too so you're aware of any new test developments.

CHAPTER 12

A Differentiating Practice Test Strategy

Let me reiterate that taking practice tests is an absolute must. What scores should you aim for on these practice tests? A basic 70 percent won't set you up as a likely passer. As usual with the CFA Program, it's more complicated than that.

Setting Practice Test Expectations and Goals

The CFA Institute has always passed any candidate making a 70 percent or better on the CFA exams. The hurdle might even be less than that. The CFA Institute decides the passing score on a test-by-test basis. Aside from passing everyone scoring a 70 percent, it might pass candidates with a 65 percent this time around because the exam is tougher. The Institute chooses the minimum score after the test is over and never announces it. Since candidates can't train for a mark they don't know exists, candidates generally work with the 70 percent target.

However, for practice tests, 70 percent shouldn't be *your* target. It's too risky because, without context, a practice exam's numerical grade is just a number. The mock exam may not reflect the real test's difficulty and therefore your score doesn't compare to how you would perform on the actual test. A good score on an easy test means little.

Unless the practice test and the real CFA test are equally difficult, a numerical grade from the practice test doesn't necessarily reveal how you might score on the CFA Institute's test. Evidencing that absolute, numerical scores are fallible, almost every candidate aims for and makes a 70 percent score on practice tests. Yet a majority don't pass the real thing. Like every other aspect of the CFA Program, if the average candidate aims for a certain goal, you should aim higher.

Before you contemplate how much higher, like most other candidates, you have a date with humility. When beginning your practice test efforts, you'll likely suffer the quintessential CFA-candidate experience of miserably failing your first attempt. It won't be pretty. I scored a 44 percent on my first Level I practice test. Even after months of studying, a 44 percent! I didn't know it then, but that's typical. Candidates generally score very low on initial exams because they wait (appropriately) until the 45-day final review period to take the first one. At that point, some topics haven't been touched in months and all subjects have only been reviewed once. You'll probably face a similarly discouraging result. Take heart. It will get better because you now have insight into what subjects stuck with you and which ones need more attention.

You move on from that first practice test with a slightly bruised ego and rattled nerves. A bad score is frightening when you are close to test day. Other candidates ask how you did, and you exaggerate by 10 points. That's okay—they're fibbing, too. Put that test in a safe place where you can refer back to it in a few weeks when you need a good laugh. Then, let the 45-day final review commence.

Days of intense studying fly by, and soon, it's time for your second practice test. You apply my recommended strategy of taking the "morning" session on a weekday and the "afternoon" session over the weekend. You study hard in between. The dedication pays off, and instead of the 45 to 50 percent from last time, you make a grade of 60 percent. That's less scary. Breathe a sigh of relief and keep chugging along. By the third practice test, you may finally score a 70 percent.

The steady improvement is praiseworthy but, unfortunately, you can't know if this score is something to celebrate or not. The practice test might not have been hard enough to reflect the CFA Institute's actual test and most other candidates would score just as high. Then again, if your grade is better than most other candidates who took that same practice test, you could be well positioned for a passing result on the real exam. All things considered, the number itself matters less than your relative standing.

It's All Relative

The best practice test ranks your performance against your peers. You might make a 70 percent but, perhaps, most candidates scored a 75 percent. Rather than bask in the glory of your 70 percent, the relative comparison shows that you've got work to do. A practice test with scores so pervasively high is unrealistic—again, a majority of candidates don't pass the CFA exams. The CFA Institute is quite good at crafting tests that only about one-third can pass, so you need to perform better than other candidates. If you're performing below two-thirds of those taking the exam, regardless of your numerical score, you're likely not in the passing segment.

Thankfully, such comparative practice tests can be found online through test prep companies. Candidates sign up with one of these third-party companies to receive both numerical scores and rankings for each practice test they take. You can complete one of these exams on a computer whenever you like and your score is added to the company's database. The vendor compares your score against all candidates who have taken the same test and provides your percentile ranking. Scoring in the 70th percentile is good; scoring in the 50th percentile is not.

You may tire of hearing this, but AnalystNotes is a good option for practice tests that benchmark your performance and do not cost a fortune. Allen Resources also compares performance for a reasonable price, although a bit differently through comparisons on groupings of questions and not standalone practice tests. Still, any comparison helps. Finally, Schweser offers a ranking service but costs an absurd $100 for a single online test. Schweser has better name recognition, but AnalystNotes and Allen Resources provide better value for your money.

These relative-scoring practice tests can be a real eye opener, as they were for me. Early in my 45-day review period for Level I, half of my fellow candidates were scoring better than me on AnalystNotes' tests. Again, majorities don't pass the CFA exams. The obvious conclusion: I would fail the real exam if I didn't improve. Never mind the score; my competition was outpacing me. This was my cue to step it up. I credit the benchmarking system for giving me that perspective. On tests that rate candidates against each other, concentrate on outperforming instead of the numerical test result.

Though these relative performance tests are beneficial for many candidates, they are exclusively online. Alas, the CFA exams aren't given on a computer. They are traditional paper and pencil exams, which online practice tests can't simulate. You might prefer paper and pencil exams because they feel more like the real thing, which makes sense.

However, a paper and pencil practice test only provides an absolute score and not a relative rank. On these absolute-scoring practice exams, let's determine what grade to pursue.

Give Yourself a Buffer

If a test isn't ranking your performance against other candidates, you must perform better than typical passing rates to make sure there's a buffer between you and that risky pass/fail line. There's no way to normalize the test's difficulty, so compensate by scoring far enough past 70 percent to counteract the uncertainty.

For Level I, settle for nothing less than 80 percent on non-ranking paper exams by the end of your test prep. Level I practice tests aren't unduly difficult and this grade is attainable. An 80 percent won't happen right away. Scores this high likely won't occur until at least your fourth attempt, and you may have to add a fifth practice exam to clinch an 80 percent score. The studying days between each test continually lift your performance so that you eventually get there. You'll be amazed at how much you improve over time.

At Level II, scoring 80 percent might not happen. Level II is extremely difficult. But, it's my opinion, and the opinion of many other candidates, that the CFA Institute sets Level II passing scores closer to 60 percent rather than 70. Therefore, lower grades may still succeed. Don't stress yourself trying to get the same scores on Level II practice tests as you did in Level I. Aim for 75 percent on your final Level II practice tests; it's only a five percent difference from 80 percent, but it will seem a world apart when you are taking Level II practice exams.

You probably won't see high scores on Level III practice tests, either. Again, target 75 percent. Scoring your Level III practice exams isn't straightforward because the essay grading is somewhat subjective. If, after comparing your answers to the answer key, you're uncertain about whether or not an answer would be accepted, be conservative and don't give yourself any points. This way, you can be more confident in your scores.

To be clear, the Level III essay questions are not asking for true essay responses. The CFA Institute doesn't even call them essay questions; they are called "constructed-response questions." You are not expected to write essays; you can (and should) use bullet points, lists, and sentence fragments where appropriate to answer these questions on the exam. However, a word of caution; don't skimp on your answers. Many test prep services encourage candidates to write only the bare minimum necessary and then move on for the sake of time. While this would make sense if a machine was scoring your answers, your responses are graded by humans. Every year, about 500 CFA charterholders gather in Charlottesville, Virginia to grade the Level III constructed-response questions. They can, and will, give partial credit if you hit the mark on parts of your answer but miss it on others. One of the graders' main goals is to determine if you are proficient enough to deserve a passing result. You may get partial credit if you demonstrate that you are on the right track.

The essay-grading process is highly controlled. Level III graders are separated into teams and assigned a certain question to grade.[21] The team is provided with an answer key for their question, which is then reviewed against actual candidate answers to make sure that full and partial credit is awarded when appropriate. Once the team's leaders have confidence in the answer key, the graders begin scoring the question. Leaders perform quality-control checks throughout the process to ensure that the questions are being graded consistently.

There are a couple important things to understand about this process. First, you won't get credit for an answer that is unrelated to the essay question. Don't deviate from the question and start regurgitating other information. However, you can get partial credit if the grader sees that you have some understanding of the concept being tested. I aimed for a happy medium when answering my Level III constructed-response questions, which worked out well for me. I answered with enough supporting information to show that I grasped the concept being tested (even if the technical parts of my response turned out to be wrong), but refrained from writing long or meandering narratives. You can usually accomplish this with only a couple bullet-point statements or a quick explanation. Also, show the equation you're using when solving math problems.

For all three Levels, try to grade your practice exams as if it is someone else's exam. It can be tempting to give yourself points for multiple-choice questions that you originally answered correctly but then changed, or award generous partial credit on essay responses that are largely flawed. If you apply restraint, you can have more faith in the realism of your practice results.

I recognize that the 80, 75, and 75 percent targets for Levels I, II, and III, respectively, are blanket statements not taking into account that available practice tests range in difficulty. Comparing practice test vendors is a common topic in online forums. These discussions can help you standardize the difficulty of your vendor's practice tests versus others. My recommendations assume the practice exams aren't incredibly difficult; if yours are, adjust your goals accordingly.

All Practice Tests Are Not Created Equal

Don't take advice suggesting that you aim for 70 percent on practice tests because the CFA Institute passes that score on the real exam. That's everybody's goal, so it shouldn't be yours.

Keep in mind that passing practice tests means little if everyone else is passing them, too. Try to find exams comparing your performance to others or, conversely, aim for high scores on absolute-scoring paper tests.

Key Takeaways: A Differentiating Practice Test Strategy

- The CFA Institute has always passed candidates making a 70 percent or higher on the CFA exams, so most candidates target this threshold on practice tests. However, the difficulty on practice tests might not equate to the real thing. Seek comparisons of your performance against other candidates or, build in a buffer and pursue a higher score.

- Candidates typically score poorly on their first practice tests, which is why you should complete at least four practice tests, not one. You'll do better with time.

- Some online providers rank your mock-exam performance against your peers. This provides great insight by revealing if you're performing above average. The numerical score means less than your relative standing.

- Printed practice exams don't benchmark your score against other candidates, but they more closely mirror the CFA exams' real-life, pen-and-paper experience. If you prefer these paper exams, try for higher scores to offset the fact that you can't know how their difficulty matches the actual test.

- On Level I practice tests that don't rank your performance, an 80 percent puts a sufficient cushion between you and the pass/fail line. You can't know how other candidates did on the same exam or how it compares to the real one, so an 80 percent offers a safety margin.

- A high score isn't likely on Level II or III practice exams; these Levels are harder. Aim for 75 percent, which is still a difficult goal.

- Practice tests are fantastic tools but must be used wisely. Either compare yourself to other candidates taking the same exams, or reach for higher numerical scores than average candidates will.

CHAPTER 13

Study Groups Are Overrated

There appear to be two factions of candidates who find comfort in the concept of a study group. There are those who are in way over their heads, and the serial procrastinators who can't be trusted to study alone. Every study group I've ever known contained at least one of each. Others in the group may become frustrated, and few get what they really need. A study group may not be the answer for any of them.

I'm Trying, but I Need Help

The CFA Program is skewed towards one learning type: independent study. However, not everyone learns the same way. With only the curriculum books and study notes as explanatory material, perhaps you're looking for someone to provide more color. There is nothing wrong with wanting verbal or visual help. A study group might seem like a fine solution.

However, in my opinion, study groups under serve this need in the long run. If you rely on a study group to get through Level I, then you're really in a pickle. The curriculum becomes much harder at Level II, while the number of candidates pursuing Level II in your geographical area becomes much smaller. The chances of having enough upper-Level candidates to form a study group are slim. The problem becomes even worse at Level III as only approximately 25,000 candidates worldwide are taking that exam.

These tests are made for people who learn well through independent study, but that doesn't mean no one else can succeed. If you feel that you need the added help of a study group—and not just as a procrastination prevention device—then, a class might be a better idea. Classes tend to be expensive, but you may simply need a teacher or tutor.

There are many available options. If you live in a metropolitan area, check out your local CFA society to see if it offers an in-person, weekly class. Many offer classes that meet once or twice each week in the months leading to test day. Additionally, big cities might have a third-party company or two offering classes.

If you don't have access to an in-person class, some large test prep services also offer online classes, which "meet" once or twice a week through a chat room. Additionally, Schweser, Allen Resources, and other vendors offer video lectures. Recorded lectures lose the teacher-student interaction, but may be worth considering. (Check out the "Test Preparation Resources" section for more information on the available class alternatives.)

With classes, you may still combat the problem of finding little support in Level III. Fielding a full class in Level III is difficult in all but the largest cities. By this point, video lectures, online classes, and tutoring are your main options. Though you may have to change the type of class you take, you can find assistance in all three Levels without a study group.

If classes or video lectures are too expensive or otherwise prohibitive, do extra practice questions. I learned a lot from the explanations given after each practice question, both in the curriculum books and from third parties. Practice questions help explain the material.

As you employ all the aids at your disposal, continually assess your comprehension. If Level I is a constant struggle, you have a far weaker likelihood of clearing Levels II and III. This may sound harsh, but the CFA Program takes your time and money. Thinking ahead can save a lot of both.

Don't quit because you're occasionally struggling. Everyone struggles in this program now and then. Many candidates who are initially perplexed in Level I markedly improve over time and go on to earn their charters. Rather, consider quitting if you can't answer at least 60 percent of practice questions correctly as you move through the material (you'll have a final review period to improve this percentage above 70 percent). If you are leaving study sessions feeling as lost as when you started, then decide if a class, tutor, or video lectures might help you achieve the 60 percent success rate on practice questions. If not, do some soul searching.

You may be unsure about your comprehension level and, relatedly, your need for study assistance. If you understand the progression of ideas in your study notes, the formulas are only occasionally confusing, and you finish the first few subjects feeling like you understand most of the material, you're in good shape. You might not understand some concepts but, as long as this is not the norm, you're almost certainly on the right path.

Notwithstanding my opinions, you must judge your comprehension for yourself. Evaluating your evolution in the CFA Program is an inherently personal issue. Whatever your conclusion, I would avoid the study group.

I'd Rather Play Video Games

Procrastinators, your predicament is trickier. Studying is tedious and temptation is everywhere. Even undesirable tasks (cleaning, paying bills, etc.) become preferable to sitting down with those curriculum books for another minute.

I completely understand the draw of procrastination. As the television now beckons me away from writing this sentence, I don't know how I resisted reaching for the remote control for months in the CFA Program. Unfortunately, procrastination is the silent killer of potential CFA charters. The only way I know how to fight procrastination is to not let it begin. In serving this purpose, a study group fails as it is a social gathering and, as such, breeds wasted time as you start taking breaks to discuss last night's sports game or reality television show. You want to reduce distractions, not introduce new ones. Don't join a group that solves one problem by creating others. The solution for a procrastination addict is not a study group.

Again, classes are an option. Classes provide structure, and you may focus better on a lecturing teacher than in a group of peers. You are expected to keep up with the class, which discourages procrastination. Although, classes contain their own distractions, such as traveling to and from class when you could be studying, or socializing before and after class begins.

As an alternative to the class and the study group, consider forming a progress group. Find a couple of candidates at your Level who may also need help in the procrastination department. Commit to checking in with each other once per week to get an update on each person's progress. If you don't know anyone in your Level, try the various CFA forums online such as www.AnalystForum.com or www.300hours.com (I list various forums, as well, in the "Test Preparation Resources" section). This is a great way to find other candidates to begin a support group. You don't need to see each other in person; simply set up a recurring video chat or conference call.

Procrastinators are not the only candidates who can find significant value in this type of progress group. For any candidate, periodic communication keeps you informed on your pace versus others. If by the second month your friends have covered eight subjects while you have completed only four, this could be a problem. Conversely, maybe they are moving too fast and your speed is appropriate. Measuring your pace in relation to others shouldn't determine your agenda, but this can be useful information as you wonder how others are approaching the six curriculum books.

Expect Lots of "Me" Time

The CFA Program is structured as an independent study course. For months, you're expected to study alone on almost a daily basis. Even with a class or other interactive tool, most hours are spent by yourself.

Some candidates acclimate easily, while others must make a determined effort to adjust.

I live in the southeastern United States where the humidity is, basically, insane. During summer, the air is so thick with water that we are essentially swimming in it instead of walking. I don't mind (and sometimes don't notice) because I grew up with the extreme humidity and am used to it. Newcomers aren't so indifferent. Some adjust favorably as the weather fits their disposition and preference. Others battle it on an ongoing basis, but they remain here for years and thrive. Lastly, some people can't take it, gladly admit the humidity is not for them, and relocate to a more suitable climate.

As with those who dislike high humidity, the CFA Program's independent study climate may not be ideal for you. Try to determine if it's something you can tolerate. You might not prefer it like some candidates, but maybe a progress group or class serves as a great dehumidifier. See if you can adjust.

A study group might also serve as a dehumidifier, but only temporarily. Joining a study group for Level I is like arriving in the southeastern United States in the winter; this tricks you into thinking the humidity is relatively tame. Both the overwhelmed candidate and the procrastinator might have serious difficulties at later Levels if they rely on a study group to get them through Level I. Learn to study independently before Levels II and III force the issue later in the Program.

Assistance is available to help candidates become successful, solitary studiers most of the time with teacher or candidate interaction sometimes. Explore the various possibilities. Most hours might be spent studying alone, but you don't have to confront the entire Program alone. Avoid seeking solace in a study group and let other alternatives help you adjust to the CFA Program's environment.

Key Takeaways: Study Groups Are Overrated

- Study groups often are not helpful and, by Levels II and III, rarely available. Learn to study independently without a study group.

- Some candidates need personal communication, while others need help with procrastination. Alternate solutions exist instead of the traditional study group.

- If you feel overwhelmed by the curriculum or like to interact with a live person while you learn, consider signing up for a class with your local CFA society or a third-party company. The classes are generally held on a weekly basis in the months leading up to the exams. You can attend a class online or in person.

- Many companies offer video lectures for purchase online. Though you won't have teacher-student interaction, an expert's insights can be useful and provide an alternative for verbal learners.

- Practice questions also help explain the material and assess your comprehension level. If, during your first pass at learning the curriculum, you can't correctly answer 60 percent of the questions from the most recent topic you covered, consider changing your approach, incorporating other aids, or pursuing another designation.

- Procrastination isn't cured by a study group. Establish a progress group instead. Agree to check in with each other once per week to discuss how far along each person has come and what you intend to accomplish in the next week.

- A progress group can serve procrastinators and non-procrastinators alike by providing an opportunity to gauge your progress against other candidates. However, don't let the group's progress determine yours.

- The CFA Program is designed for independent studying, but this does not mean you are completely alone. Alternatives to the study group can help you succeed while supporting your independent study time.

CHAPTER 14

Read This When You Want to Quit

Looking back, even after writing an entire book on the CFA Program, I have zero nostalgia for the Program or my studying days. I will not suggest that you should appreciate this experience or that you should, on some level, enjoy the grueling but special education you're receiving! No, the CFA Program is not particularly enjoyable. Unlike many other educational endeavors (college, graduate school, etc.), this program promises no leisurely weekends or classmate bonding. The Program can wear you down.

You're past exhausted ... you're so tired that you're angry about it. When you finally lay down to sleep, the material runs through your head in circles. Those blasted study books. Can you please get five minutes respite from those relentless books?! They haunt every minute of your life.

Your loved ones are starting to lose patience with your singular focus on something called "the CFA Program." They might not say it directly, but they'll suggest that you keep your agony to yourself. After all, they're just tests! Of course, your family and friends support you, but you are starting to feel isolated.

This is a lonely endeavor. I believe that charterholders would fare better than most people in solitary confinement; we've had practice. A social life rarely co-exists with a passing CFA-exam score, particularly in the last few weeks before test day. Sacrifices must be made and, unfortunately, the day's 24 hours are only sufficient to contain work, CFA studying, and sleep. I saw my friends and family during the CFA Program, but sparingly. Some will appreciate why you've become a hermit, while others will have no grasp of why you willingly lock yourself in a room to study until you fall asleep. In a few years, they will see what the CFA charter has done for your career, your family, and your life and, eventually, understand.

Now, though, with the test still months away and the foreign-exchange chapters reading like gibberish, you are entertaining thoughts of quitting. You want to walk away from this program and never look back. You'd read a book for pleasure or watch all the television shows you've been missing. Perhaps tomorrow's lunch hour could be spent with people instead of flashcards. Maybe a vacation is in order. You can almost hear a white, sandy beach calling your name.

You're understandably drained. Pursuing the CFA charter is like climbing a steep, massive, punishing mountain, and you need to reach the summit before the storm clouds roll in. You've heard that most hikers never make it to the mountain's peak. You constantly second guess your progress. You are a degree of tired that you didn't think was possible. You were expecting a tough climb, but this is something else.

Mountain climbing is a curious thing. Mountaineers liken it to a physically-demanding chess match that requires mental resolve as much as physical stamina. In particular, peaks are visually tricky; you can be sure that it is right there, until you turn a corner and discover you've got another 1,000 feet to climb. The three classic rules of mountaineering proclaim: It's always further than it looks. It's always taller than it looks. And it's always harder than it looks. This can be an unclear, hazy ordeal that is different from most challenges. There is no set race distance that promises a precise end, or a game with timed periods. You can't know what, exactly, lies ahead on the mountain until after you've reached the summit. You are constantly racing the clock and pressing forward, even as you discover new obstacles that try to set you back.

It's said that one of the hardest parts of any climb is the half-way point; you're exhausted but lots of exertion remains. Each step feels like an agonizing, extraordinary effort. Many climbers will glance over a half-way outlook, decide this is the end of their journey, and turn back.

How to keep climbing when so many candidates are, at this very moment, quitting? This is typically a matter of personality. You might have the tenacity to dig in your heels and see it through the finish. Or, like me, maybe you don't know how to quit. Particularly during Level II, I desperately wanted to quit and proclaimed to anyone who would listen that tomorrow I would be free. But when tomorrow came, I begrudgingly trudged on. Sometimes, this tendency to persevere in a seemingly hopeless situation is to an individual's detriment. But, other times, what appears hopeless is not.

Keep climbing. You can conquer this mountain. This book can act as your guide, but it is your determination that will make the biggest difference. If you're willing and able to persevere, the mountain offers an amazing reward. The view at the summit is the greatest thing about mountain climbing, and you are getting closer every day. As Bree Loewen, an accomplished mountaineer, once said, "The greatest skill I ever had was being able to suffer for long periods of time. In exchange, I got to see some amazing things." Passing Levels I, II, and III are each amazing views from impressive summits. After each one, you become a tougher, sharper climber. By the end, you are one tough finance professional who *earned* the CFA charter through daily sacrifice. And the fact that you earned it makes the final view as a CFA charterholder even more satisfying.

Though it may feel bleak at times, the CFA Program can be conquered. The Program has one beautiful, merciful trait—almost anyone can pass. Anyone. These are not IQ tests. Obviously an ability to learn is a basic prerequisite of the Program but, frankly, the answers are right there in the books. You can do this. Give it enough effort and you can be successful. Many other candidates won't resist another hour playing video games or one more episode of their favorite television program. They will fail and you will stand triumphant. This course is not about determining who is a finance genius and who is not—it is about determining who has greater willpower. If you have the willpower, you can pass.

To muster renewed commitment, think forward to when the curriculum books are collecting dust on a shelf having not been cracked in years. In the throes of the Program, it's easy to forget that the rest of your life will not be spent studying derivative-pricing equations. Your years will be spent enjoying the rewards from your effort.

Eventually, this whole experience will be nothing but a painful memory. Then, like a mountain climber who keeps his first pair of hiking boots, you'll never be able to throw away your curriculum books. Even after all the pain and exhaustion they caused, the curriculum books are a physical reminder—more than the pretty charter hanging on the wall—that you chose an uncommon, challenging path and saw that path to the end.

You won't view your books with nostalgia. More like devices of torture. But, for some reason, you won't be able to let them go. Right now you probably can't imagine such thoughts as you ponder how good it would feel to rip apart each page one by one. Go ahead and fantasize the myriad ways you would go about destroying the books. Like the Program itself, those feelings will subside.

But not today. Today, you may be downright *over it*. I have no magic solution to your weariness. I hope that you can take some solace in the fact that many other CFA charterholders felt this way yet reached their summits. Remember, if this were easy, it wouldn't set you apart. You are pursuing a very special designation and you've already come so far. Refuse to give up. Keep climbing. The peak is there. Keep climbing until you arrive at the top and take in the magnificent view that you earned.

Then, pitch your tent and take a well-deserved nap.

Key Takeaways: Read This When You Want to Quit

- You can do this! The CFA Program is a mountain; keep climbing. Put one foot in front of the other until you reach the summit and take in the view as a CFA charterholder.

CHAPTER 15

Test Day Suggestions

The CFA exams are held on the same Saturday in June around the world (the Level I exam is held again in December). Each is six hours long and has two testing sessions: morning and afternoon. In most testing facilities, the morning session begins at 9:00 a.m. and concludes at noon. There is a two hour lunch break. The afternoon session begins at 2:00 p.m. with the test ending at 5:00 p.m. You will sit in an uncomfortable chair spaced roughly three feet away from the nearest candidate and answer finance questions all day.

That's the simple explanation. As you've probably grown accustomed to with the CFA Program, there is more to it. Let's walk through the day.

Before the Test Begins

Everyone will tell you to get plenty of rest the night before the exam. I wonder if they would fall immediately asleep knowing months of work are culminating in the next 24 hours. Realistically, you won't sleep well. No one does, yet candidates still pass the exams every year. Don't worry if you were counting on eight hours of sleep but end up with three. Adrenaline will carry you through the day.

Set your alarm clock to allow for travel to the testing facility and arrival at the designated testing room no later than 7:30 a.m. Treat this as a hard deadline—this provides extra time to absorb any travel disruptions, and there are more preparation tasks to be done at the testing facility before the exam starts at 9:00. If driving, set aside ample time for parking. In certain locations, hundreds of candidates may arrive to park their cars at the same time. This is typically an orderly process, but it can be slow.

You'll enter the building to find that the testing room doors are locked. They will remain locked until a few minutes before 9:00. For now, try to find a quiet space to review study material. Warming up with flashcards or practice questions is extremely important. Just think of it as stretching your mind as you would your muscles before playing a sport. Professional athletes, even after years of repetition of the most fundamental skills, show up early on game day to warm up and practice the basics. You should warm up, too.

For the morning's brief review, choose materials that cover numerous subjects without too much detail. Personally, I drilled flashcards. Whatever you pick, get the mental juices flowing. Meanwhile, there will be tons of other candidates milling about—everywhere.

Suddenly, the pass/fail statistics have faces. Each candidate is painfully aware that roughly two-thirds of those around them will fail, which creates a nervous energy. Who will it be? Will I make the cut? Conversations are kept to a low murmur while candidates steal glances at each other. They size up the competition while pretending not to.

To feel less on display, many candidates participate in odd herd behavior that most resembles giraffes (one of my favorite zoo animals). Giraffes move in herds, but the term "herd" may be overstating it. Giraffe herds are so loosely assembled that the collection looks like a coincidence rather than a purposeful unit. Giraffes like their personal space. They rarely acknowledge each other and have no leaders. Herd members have little sense of loyalty to the herd or to any other herd member, and they are perfectly willing to ditch their current troupe to join another without either group acknowledging the change. A loose collection of other giraffes is all that any single giraffe requires. Each giraffe may prefer to be alone but, more instinctually, each needs to be part of a group.

Candidates form similar herds on test day. Groups begin forming about an hour prior to test time without any explicit communication. Candidates seem to attract each other based on preferred pre-test activity. Coffee drinkers assemble together near the closest coffee source. Nervous candidates stand near the testing door. The cool kids stand far from the door to show their indifference. These impromptu group members purposefully stand apart from each other to convey their supposed independence, while still participating in herd behavior. Like giraffes, candidates want to be left alone—but not so alone as to stand out.

The brave few review flashcards, meditate, stretch, or pursue other non-group approved activities alone, while the herds covertly stare at them until the test doors are finally opened.

I was one of these exiled giraffes. My test day procedures won me lots of confused stares … and they also helped win me a CFA charter. Remember that almost everyone in your testing room will never attain a CFA designation. Being different isn't such a bad thing. Don't joint the herds.

As you sit alone reviewing the curriculum, there will be many eyes on you; ignore them. Studying at the testing facility is an activity that wins you judgmental stares as everyone assumes you are either dumb or unprepared. But, you should not enter this complicated test with a cold brain.

One of my test day experiences involved this idea of studying before the test and occurred at Level II. I sat on the floor outside of the testing room reviewing flashcards before the test began. An acquaintance from my college days approached me flanked by identically dressed wingmen.

"If you don't know it by now, you're not going to know it," he informed me with a smug smirk. Wow, thank you for that insightful observation! I smiled, shrugged, and resumed reviewing my flashcards. The test began 30 minutes later.

These exams have a mid-day break and, similar to the previous year, I hung back to wait for the rest of the test takers to rush the door as they exited for lunch—another lesson in herd behavior. Finally I left the room and, lo and behold, sitting there on the floor outside the room was the smug man surrounded by study materials and cramming his notes. Clearly he had struggled through the morning session and was trying to overcome his lack of preparation during lunch. He looked up at me and froze. Would my parents have urged me to be the bigger person? Sure. But I couldn't resist.

"If you don't know it by now, you're not going to know it," I said as I turned and walked away. I haven't seen him since. He failed Level II and dropped out of the Program.

Some won't approve, but studying before the test is a good idea. Everyone has their pre-test activities, though most people will just stand around. Use this time to kick start your brain and focus.

I'm often asked if candidates should avoid coffee or tea before the exam. I say it depends on your attachment to coffee or tea. If you can't function without it, have a cup. I wouldn't blame you—I like my morning coffee. For myself, I weighed the pluses and minuses and eventually settled on having one cup of coffee before each test. I then took one restroom break during the morning session, granted, at a near sprint. There are no rules against speed walking to the bathroom, though I probably looked silly. I didn't care since, particularly at Levels II and III, candidates might need every second of the testing time to finish. When I took those tests, almost no one finished early including me. So drinking a natural diuretic is probably not your best bet given that going to the restroom will eat up time. On the other hand, missing one question because you ran out of time is better than missing dozens because your brain was groggy all morning. It's your call. Either way, you may get up during the exam sessions if you follow the test administrators' instructions for doing so; you are not expected to sit glued to your chair for three hours. Just keep in mind that the clock is ticking.

As 9:00 rolls around, put your study materials away and gather the items that you're taking into the testing room. The CFA Institute is very strict on what you can bring into the room. No cell phones, papers, backpacks, purses, and the list goes on.[22] The testing facility provides an area to store your items, and you will have access to your items during the lunch break. Don't expect this area to be secure. With dozens and potentially hundreds of candidates piling on, the storage area starts to look like a buffet of office supplies and personal knickknacks. If possible, leave valuables in your car or at home.

While you can't bring many things inside, some items you must. The multiple choice tests are taken with pencils and erasers, which won't be provided. You must bring your own, as well as pens with blue or black ink if taking Level III's morning essay session. Don't forget your admission ticket, which you will print off from the CFA Institute's website a few days prior. The Institute also requires photo identification, and it will only accept an international passport as proof of your identity regardless of your nationality or location. The Institute is not kidding around about this policy and will turn you away without a current international passport. Make sure you have one.

A calculator is not required, but it might as well be. More on calculators later.

Aside from the required necessities, the CFA Institute publishes a laundry list of items that are permitted in the testing room at the candidate's discretion. Some items that were allowed when I took the CFA tests were ear plugs, extra pencils, jackets, calculators, watches, glasses, contact solution, medications, and tissues. Please check the current rules before assuming what items are allowed, but take advantage of what items are permissible and bring all that you could conceivably need.

This is a long, stressful day, and you don't want something as simple as a headache ruining it when you could have taken some aspirin. If debris gets on your contact lenses, take them out and wear your glasses. If your neighbor insists on breathing like a panting dog, wear the ear plugs.

By the end of three (or more) exams, most charterholders have stories of test day troubles. For my Level I exam, the room was an icebox. It could have snowed in there. The cold temperature was the talk of the lunch break; everyone was miserable. Unless candidates brought a jacket (or three), there was nothing to do but shiver. To be safe, dress in layers and bring extras.

Likewise, at Level III, my pencil stash came in handy. I went through four broken pencil tips and two useless erasers. I swear that it was like my pencils were plotting against me. Luckily, I brought ten, sharpened and ready.

Be advised that the CFA Institute doesn't allow you to carry these items in any kind of packaging. They believe that the noise of opening a pill bottle or pencil package will disrupt the other candidates around you, and they have a good point. But you can't even carry the items in a bag or container. Be prepared to walk in with your hands full. Yes, the herd will look up to stare as you balance a convenience store's worth of items in your arms. But when they see you sitting in the Level III section in a couple years, they might reconsider.

You've stowed your personal items in the storage area and gathered the items you're bringing into the testing room. Now the fun starts.

"You May Begin"

The test doors open approximately 20 minutes before 9:00. To gain admission, test proctors inspect your calculator, personal items, and admission ticket at the door. Don't try to sneak anything past these administrators. They are wise to candidates' tricks and, if caught, can end your CFA-test day right then and there. Don't risk it.

Inside, each testing facility is different. Candidates might sit together in one giant room or be divided into smaller ones. I took my exams in Atlanta, Georgia in the United States. In that testing facility, candidates assemble in one giant space that feels like the inside of a massive airplane hangar. The room is divided into three seating sections: Level I, Level II, and Level III. Tables are arranged in rows in each section. Find your Level, provide your photo ID at the check-in table (again, a current international passport), submit your calculator for a second inspection, and take your seat. Dump your personal items under your chair. Set your calculator and pencils on your desk, and wait.

A word on calculators—the CFA Institute only allows two calculator models inside the testing room. In all the known universe of calculators, candidates can test with one of these two or none at all. Candidates may use the Texas Instruments® BA II Plus™ or the Hewlett Packard® HP-12C™ (and their variants such as the "Professional" or "Anniversary" editions). Don't bother showing up with anything else since the door guards will just direct you back out to the storage area to dispose of the rejected calculator.

Use one of these two approved calculators in the months leading up to the test. When you register for Level I, acquire a calculator on the same day. Become comfortable with it during your study months to avoid struggling with an unfamiliar gadget on test day.

If possible, I suggest purchasing two approved calculators if you have the monetary means to do so or find a second one from a friend who has taken the CFA exams before. You're allowed to bring an extra calculator into the test, which I recommend. Be prepared if one quits working so you aren't faced with the alternative of failing the exam and waiting six months to a year to take it again. You can bring spare batteries instead of another calculator, but replacing the batteries in financial calculators is not a quick process. Also, calculators can have other issues beyond dead batteries. You need a calculator that works *now*.

Though my extra calculator didn't save my day, it certainly saved someone else's day. At Level I, my testing neighbor was in a serious predicament. He had flown to the testing center because he didn't live in the area. He packed his calculator in his checked luggage, which the airline lost. This poor soul was now without a calculator. He spent the morning driving to every open store looking for an approved calculator. None were stocked.

Yes, he should have kept his calculator with him when he boarded the plane. We all make mistakes. I happened to be awash in calculators that year and had three. I offered one, for which he was profusely grateful.

I finished the afternoon portion of the test with some time to spare and decided to leave without waiting for my neighbor to finish his exam and return my calculator. The following year at Level II, I felt a tap on my shoulder and turned to see the same man again as my neighbor. This time, we were both at Level II! He had passed. He thanked me again and handed over my calculator from the year before. He insisted on returning it "to its rightful owner." I still have that calculator and smile every time I see it. No, having an extra calculator didn't save my day, but it could have. And saving someone else's day felt pretty good.

Now you're ready to go with pencils, erasers, and two calculators on your desk with anything else you might need under your chair. After a few minutes, all candidates have found their seats and the test proctors call the room to order.

Before you may open your test booklet, the head supervisor reads instructions from a written script to ensure that every person hears the same message in every testing facility around the globe.

You sign a pledge swearing not to divulge the details of the test you're about to take. You go through the slow procedure of bubbling in your personal information on a standardized sheet.

Then, without further ado, the supervisor announces, "You may begin."

Three hours later, you're dismissed for lunch. The CFA Institute allows two hours for lunch because, at many testing centers, lunch options may not be right there for the taking. Two hours is plenty of time, but lunch won't be sitting outside of the testing room door.

My main lunch time advice is to eat alone. Socializing can break your focus or make you feel unmotivated to continue the afternoon's three-hour ordeal. It is not as imperative that you study during this time as it was in the morning. Review study materials, if you like, or sit quietly to give your mind a break.

Return to the testing room about 20 minutes before 2:00 p.m., which is when the afternoon session starts. Candidates show identification again and retake their seats. The test proctors read from their afternoon script and start the timer.

When you finish your test, you're not necessarily allowed to leave the room and go home. If you finish with significant time to spare, you will likely be permitted to turn in your test and leave early. If you miss the supervisor's preannounced cutoff time, you must stay in your seat and wait for 5:00 p.m. The limit may change, but during my exams, administrators prevented anyone from leaving the room after 4:30 p.m. This rule prevents commotion for those still working in the last 30 minutes, which will be almost everyone. You shouldn't try to finish as quickly as possible just so you can leave. Answer each question with appropriate thought and attention; when the 30-minute warning approaches, let it lapse.

Before long, the test proctors announce that time is up. They collect your test and send you on your way. To heck with herd behavior—you rush the door with everyone else. You're happy to get out of there and start your post-test celebration!

An Important Day like This One Needs a Plan

Strategize your test day like you do everything else in the CFA Program. Be willing to step outside standard practice and do whatever you can to have the best exam day that you can.

It's a long day. Test days are nerve-racking and intimidating but, if you have prepared for both test day and the test itself, you'll do fine. And test day is great for one key reason: when it's done, you're done!

Key Takeaways: Test Day Suggestions

- Know your test day schedule. The CFA tests occur on a Saturday with two testing sessions: morning and afternoon. The morning session typically lasts from 9:00 a.m. to 12:00 p.m. The afternoon session lasts from 2:00 p.m. to 5:00 p.m.

- Arrive outside the testing room's door by 7:30 a.m. to review study materials. Wake up your brain to the CFA material and get in a test-taking mindset. Don't worry about the other candidates around you or their opinions on pre-test studying.

- Consider the pros and cons of drinking coffee or tea. You might run out of time because you took bathroom breaks, but you might need the caffeine to wake up. The potential for missing one or two questions might be worth the risk. It's a personal choice.

- Remember to bring your required test day items: pencils (and pens for Level III), erasers, international passport, and admission ticket.

- Adhere to the CFA Institute's strict rules on what discretionary items are allowed in the testing room. Bring every approved item that you may possibly need. Remember to ditch the packaging before trying to enter the testing room.

- Consider carrying two approved calculators into the test. The CFA Institute only allows the Texas Instruments BA II Plus or the Hewlett Packard 12C. Use one of these two calculators to study until test day, and then bring two of the same brand with you.

- Eat alone during the mid-day break. Avoid socializing so that you can focus when returning for the afternoon session.

- Resist the temptation to finish your test as fast as possible. If you finish 30 minutes or more before 5:00 p.m., you are usually allowed to leave the testing room to go home. Otherwise, you must wait until the test ends. Don't try to meet the early deadline; concentrate on the test and answer each question carefully.

- Breathe a sigh of relief when the test ends. Enjoy your Saturday night—you've earned a celebration!

CHAPTER 16

Putting It All Together

We've covered a lot of ground. Schedules, flashcards, practice tests, curriculum books, study notes, and more. Now, we bring everything together into an executable study regimen.

Recall from Chapter 8, "A Study Plan from Start to Finish," that studying for a CFA test is like managing a project. There are two critical-path phases that govern your study activities: a 14-week (three-and-a-half month) initial study phase followed by a 45-day review period.

Let's pretend that you're taking the June exam in a few months. It is mid-January and you're ready to set off on your initial 14-week study phase. You've bought your CFA Institute-approved calculator. You've set aside 15 study hours each week for the next three-and-a-half months. You've coordinated an appropriate mid-

April start to your subsequent review period and are prepared to study more in those final days.

Before you begin, plan out the first critical-phase path on a calendar. Lay out exactly what study sessions you'll complete on what days during the next 14 weeks. Refer to the week-by-week sample calendars that I provide in the resources section, as well as the CFA Institute's topic weighting matrix from Chapter 4, "The Second Secret to Passing CFA Exams." Use the sample schedules and matrix to help you design a schedule that works for you.

In scheduling the 18 study sessions, rearrange them as you see fit; you don't have to adhere to the curriculum books' order. Corporate Finance might be study session 11, but maybe it makes more sense to review that topic first. Or, Economics could be session 4 but you schedule it in week 11. Candidates can adjust the order because most topics stand on their own.

There are some instances where you should keep readings together that go together (for example, there might be two study sessions on Equity Investments that shouldn't be split up) but, aside from a few instances, the curriculum is flexible. Even those study sessions classified under an umbrella term, such as "asset classes," don't interact. The only one I wouldn't rearrange is Wealth Management as it draws on the other subjects; let it remain a late-stage topic. Otherwise, schedule as you please.

As you reshuffle the study sessions, consider tackling smaller-weighted topics in the first couple weeks while you're getting accustomed to the Program. As the exception, study Ethics—a very important topic—early and often.

After a couple weeks spent with smaller topics, move into the thick of the curriculum. You might schedule two weeks for the larger, weightier subjects, while one week suffices for most and some take only a couple days. Flipping through the curriculum books and pondering the topic matrix can help you make these scheduling choices. Don't be too exact in planning exactly what you'll do each and every day. Generalities are fine: "I'll study Quantitative Methods this week and Fixed Income next." This way, you have a schedule but it's adaptable.

Now that you have your study plan for the next few months, fire up the study engine.

A Repeatable Outline for the next 14 Weeks

While scheduling every minute of study activity isn't productive—life will change the exact schedule—a weekly outline helps organize your time.

Most weeks follow a consistent pattern as most study sessions have comparable sizes. On Monday, begin each study session by reading for a few hours. Remember that you can heavily rely on study notes in Level I, but the curriculum books should rule your days in Levels II and III. As you read through the study session, make flashcards. Also, pay close attention to any example problems in the texts. Continue in this way Tuesday through Friday. When finished reading, you'll have a hefty mound of flashcards (approximately 25) and conceptual knowledge of the topic as you head into the weekend.

Devote your weekend study hours to turning that conceptual knowledge into concrete knowledge. Answer practice questions on Saturday. Find them at the end of each chapter in the curriculum books, online in the CFA Institute's topic-based quizzes, and through your chosen third-party provider.

For Level I, complete approximately 75 practice questions for a typical study session. Many of these will be quick, one- or two-line questions, so the large volume isn't as overwhelming as it sounds. By answering plenty of practice questions, you have a high likelihood of testing yourself on all of the major concepts that were presented throughout the study session.

In Levels II and III, practice questions tend to be longer and the total volume is smaller. Consider answering 50 practice questions for each Level II study session. Answer about 40 practice questions in each study session in Level III, many of which will be in essay form.

On Sunday, review the study session's flashcards once. Don't blast through these. Take your time and let the flashcards hammer the study session into your brain so you can recall the information months from now.

When Sunday comes to a close, you should be finished with that study session. Tomorrow, on to the next.

For some candidates, this outline of studying every day, all week is too relentless. If you need at least one day off each week for religious reasons or to give your brain a break, assign extra time on the other days. As long as you study enough total hours, you can have a free day.

Notice that I didn't mention a study group in laying out this weekly plan. They usually waste time. Instead, if you like, fold a class or progress group into the framework. Classes typically meet once per week and cover one topic at each meeting, so this fits with the above approach. Once you obtain the class calendar, you can coordinate yours with the class schedule.

If you don't need the teacher interaction, consider a progress group to keep informed on how fast other candidates are moving through the material. The progress group also helps keep any procrastination tendencies in check.

As Monday rolls around again, repeat the process with the next study session. Some weeks, you might complete these tasks faster to cover two smaller study sessions in one week. No matter the length, do the same activities for every session: read, study examples, make flashcards, complete practice questions, and review flashcards.

Normal life interrupts your agenda now and then; when the interruption ends, work harder to get back on track. Do whatever is necessary to finish that first 14-week round of studying on time. Respect the 45-day review date as the law.

Six Weeks of Digging Deep

Now, the 45-day review period begins. Scheduling is critical during this phase, which consists of two stages itself: a 40-day review of everything you covered in the last few months followed by a five-day sprint to home plate.

Break out your calendar again. Over 40 days, allot two or three to each study session. For instance, review Economics on Monday and Tuesday, Quantitative Methods on Wednesday, Thursday, and Friday, and Alternative Investments over the weekend. During this time, reexamine your notes, redo dozens of practice problems, and drill flashcards. Remember to review each study sessions' flashcards twice in succession before moving on to the next.

At some point, you'll probably run out of new practice questions. Your third-party vendor, the curriculum books, and the CFA Institute only have so many. Recycle ones you've already answered. This helps you remember them later and is a good exercise to help decipher the nuanced questions.

Six weeks is a tight timetable to cover *lots* of material. With so much to do in such short timeframes, precisely plan each and every day. There's not much time for flexibility or generalities now; the daily schedule should be specific to make sure you get everything done in time for the exam.

Adding to the load, you also need to take four practice exams. Schedule these into your calendar, taking one at the beginning of the 40-day review period and one towards the end. Split the other two along the morning and afternoon sessions—making four mini-tests—and sprinkle them throughout the middle weeks. Aim for an 80 percent on your last practice test in Level I and 75 percent in Levels II and III. Four practice tests is a guideline. If needed, take extra to meet your goal.

By design, your intensity level must increase during these final weeks. Double your commitment to 30 hours per week in Level I and more in Levels II and III. Assuming you have a day job, you're now working constantly. It's straining, but it's relatively brief. This is the toughest part of the Program but also the most decisive. Hunker down and keep going.

The final week arrives and it's a flurry of activity. Shore up any concepts that are giving you trouble. Revisit flashcards that you're still tripping over. Review Ethics again—your fourth repetition at least—with another cover-to-cover reading of the Ethics handbook and a few dozen practice problems.

On Friday night, assemble your test day items and discard any packaging. Collect whatever flashcards or study material you'll review on Saturday morning before the test begins. Eat a good meal, set two alarm clocks, and try to sleep.

A Holistic Plan Is the Key to Success

By combining the tools, strategies, and suggestions from previous chapters into a plan you feel comfortable implementing, you can clear a path to the CFA designation. If you manage your

CFA project every step of the way, you can succeed and become a CFA charterholder.

We can debate the merits of various study note providers, or the value of previous industry experience, or how many practice tests to take. In the end, time management matters most. What a relief! Manage your time well and everything else falls into place. You've got a solid plan. Now ... execute.

Key Takeaways: Putting It All Together

- Bear in mind the two critical-path segments that make up your CFA project: a 14-week initial study phase followed by a 45-day review period.

- For the 14-week period, pencil the 18 study sessions into your calendar according to length and weight. Tackle the smaller-weighted topics first as you familiarize yourself with the Program. Then, digest the meat of the curriculum, adjusting your daily activities as needed to keep the overall agenda on track.

- Study the topics one by one. For each study session, read the material, concentrate on examples, and make flashcards. Complete roughly 75 practice problems. Review the flashcards for that study session once, and then move on to the next session.

- Divide the final 45-day review period into two stages: a 40-day review of the entire curriculum followed by a five-day finale. Increase your intensity so you can be ready for test day.

- During this second review period, reexamine your notes, review practice problems, drill flashcards, and take practice tests. Aim for 80 percent on your last mock exam in Level I and 75 percent in Levels II and III.

- In the last five days, reinforce challenging concepts, reexamine difficult flashcards, and cover Ethics one more time.

- Organize your test-day items on Friday night before the test. Set aside some light study materials to review in the morning before the test begins at 9:00 a.m. Awake early and greet test day knowing that you are prepared.

- Manage your time carefully throughout the CFA Program. Time management issues bring down candidates every year, but with a solid plan, you can succeed.

FINAL THOUGHTS

You've reached the end of this book, which is really the beginning of your journey. The CFA Program awaits.

The road ahead might become draining and frustrating at times, but it's also inspiring and liberating. You're going to do something that matters! You're embarking on an important, consequential journey, and that is a beautiful thing.

We've spent many pages together constructing a solid map to guide you through the three CFA Levels. You've read about tools and strategies that can deliver passing results. You know how many candidates pass and why. You're armed with knowledge on what the English testing language means for you. You realize that Ethics has more sway than it first appears. You brush off any lack of industry experience, or you're ready to study hard even if you're a finance veteran. You understand that studying only 300 hours is a dangerous game. You know how to integrate practice questions, flashcards, curriculum books, notes, and mock exams into your study regimen. You are considering a class or progress group, but plan to avoid the study group. You appreciate that heavier-weighted topics deserve generous attention, while no topic can be ignored.

I hope that *Direct Path to the CFA Charter* helps you avoid the many hours I spent searching for CFA-testing insights that translate to successful results. My goal has been to help you pass the CFA exams in the most reliable, efficient manner possible, and now you are armed with a sound plan for making your CFA dream a reality. I hope you feel confident as you open your CFA-study materials each day, because you know proven, effective strategies for attaining the CFA charter and are doing the hard work to earn it.

We've covered many things, but most important is the principle that underlies this entire book: you must commit. These methods can make a huge difference, but only if you substantiate them with steady effort. This is not the time for wishy-washy indecision. If you choose the CFA path, march down it. Take each step with purpose and resolve. Remember that dedication goes farther than any piece of advice I can give.

We get few opportunities in life to do something grand—to accomplish something deserving of others' pride and respect, and our own. Gaining the CFA charter is such an opportunity. This will be one of your career's biggest challenges, but it can also be one of your biggest accomplishments.

I tip my hat to you, CFA candidate. Knowing the odds and difficulties ahead, you devote yourself nonetheless. Few others are willing to challenge themselves so thoroughly in the professional world. I commend you. Better yet, commend yourself.

I sincerely thank you for spending this time with me learning the direct path to the CFA charter. It has been a pleasure and honor to serve you and see your CFA journey onwards. I will be rooting for your success, and I look forward to welcoming you as a new CFA charterholder!

Cheers,
Rachel Bryant, CFA
rachel@rachel-bryant.com

LEVEL I RECAP AND SAMPLE SCHEDULE

Key Features of the Level I Exam:

- Builds a foundation in 10 investing-related topics. The topics weights are generally stable, with the heaviest ones belonging to Financial Reporting and Analysis (20 percent), Ethics (15 percent), Quantitative Methods (12 percent), and Fixed Income (12 percent).

- Offered twice per year in June and December. The exam is six hours long, with a break in the middle.

- Presents 240 multiple-choice questions, with 120 questions in the morning session and 120 questions in the afternoon.

Strategies for Passing Level I:

- Review the Ethics handbooks at least four times before test day. Complete 100 practice questions the first time you study Ethics, and answer a few dozen more during your final 45-day review period.

- Study at least 350 hours (400 hours if you are not native to the English language). If you study more than the average candidate, you are more likely to pass the exam.

- Consider taking the Level I exam in June rather than December to help your prospects for Level II.

- If you take the December exam and plan to take Level II the following June, start studying Level II third-party resources as you wait for test results, or plan to study intensely for a few weeks in February to catch up.

- Study 15 hours per week during the first 14-week study phase in Level I. You might study roughly 10 hours during the work week and another five over the weekend for a total of 15 each week.

- Utilize the curriculum books' practice questions and Ethics handbooks, even if you decide to rely more heavily on third-party study notes rather than curriculum readings.

- Make roughly 300 flashcards as you move through the material. This equates to about 17 flashcards per study session.

- Answer about 1,500 practice questions during the 14-week study period. This equates to about 75 practice questions per study session; many are short multiple-choice questions that can be answered quickly.

- Plan to study 25 hours per week in the last 45 days before test day. During this time, take four practice tests (seven if lacking command of the English language) and review study notes, practice questions, and flashcards for every study session.

- Aim for 80 percent scores on practice tests. Consider using a service that ranks your performance against other candidates taking the same exam.

- Use the last five days to review Ethics one final time, review any trouble spots, and drill flashcards.

Week-by-Week Sample Schedule
Level I

January

MONDAY	TUESDAY	WEDNESDAY	THURSDAY	FRIDAY	SATURDAY	SUNDAY
		1	2	3	4	5
6	7	8	9	10	11	12
13	14	15	16	17	18	19
Corporate Finance (session 11)				Alternative Investments (session 18)		
20	21	22	23	24	25	26
Ethics (session 1)						
27	28	29	30	31		
Economics (session 4)						

February

MONDAY	TUESDAY	WEDNESDAY	THURSDAY	FRIDAY	SATURDAY	SUNDAY
					1	2
					Economics (session 4)	
3	4	5	6	7	8	9
Economics (5 & 6)						
10	11	12	13	14	15	16
Quantitative Methods (2)						
17	18	19	20	21	22	23
Quantitative Methods (3)						
24	25	26	27	28		
Financial Reporting and Analysis (7 & 8)						

March

MONDAY	TUESDAY	WEDNESDAY	THURSDAY	FRIDAY	SATURDAY	SUNDAY
					1	2
					Financial R & A (7 & 8)	
3	4	5	6	7	8	9
Financial Reporting and Analysis (9)						
10	11	12	13	14	15	16
Financial Reporting and Analysis (10)						
17	18	19	20	21	22	23
Equity Investments (13)						
24	25	26	27	28	29	30
Equity Investments (14)				Vacation!		
31						
Vacation!						

April

MONDAY	TUESDAY	WEDNESDAY	THURSDAY	FRIDAY	SATURDAY	SUNDAY
	1	2	3	4	5	6
Fixed Income (15)						
7	8	9	10	11	12	13
Fixed Income (16)						
14	15	16	17	18	19	20
Derivatives (17)			Portfolio Management (12)			Mock Test 1
21	22	23	24	25	26	27
2nd Review: Corporate Finance			Alternative Investments		Derivatives	
28	29	30				
Ethics						

May

MONDAY	TUESDAY	WEDNESDAY	THURSDAY	FRIDAY	SATURDAY	SUNDAY
			1	2	3	4
				Economics		Mock 2 Half
5	6	7	8	9	10	11
Economics		Mock 2 Half	Quantitative Methods			
12	13	14	15	16	17	18
Financial Reporting and Analysis						Mock 3 Half
19	20	21	22	23	24	25
Financial Reporting/Analysis		Mock 3 Half	Equity Investments			
26	27	28	29	30	31	
Fixed Income				Portfolio Management		

June

MONDAY	TUESDAY	WEDNESDAY	THURSDAY	FRIDAY	SATURDAY	SUNDAY
						1
						Mock Test 4
2	3	4	5	6	7	8
Final Review: Trouble Spots, Ethics, and Flashcards					Test Day!	

LEVEL II RECAP AND SAMPLE SCHEDULE

Key Features of the Level II Exam:

- Focuses on real-world application of the same 10 testing topics from Level I. However, the difficulty and expected proficiency are much higher.

- Gives topic weights in ranges instead of precise weights, with the exception of Ethics, which is weighted 10 percent. The largest-weighted topics are Financial Reporting and Analysis (15 to 25 percent) and Equity Investments (20 to 30 percent).

- Retires certain topics after Level II that will not appear on the Level III exam: Corporate Finance, Quantitative Methods, and Financial Reporting and Analysis.

- Offered once per year in June, which means failing candidates must wait a year to repeat the Level.

- Presents 120 multiple-choice questions which accompany vignettes (short narratives). Each vignette contains a few paragraphs of information and is followed by six multiple-choice questions related to what you just read.

Strategies for Passing Level II:

- Study at least 500 hours (550 if not native to the English language). The Level II exam is very challenging and the Level II candidate pool has demonstrated itself to be more adept. Only about 40 percent will pass the exam, so you must outperform the average candidate.

- Prepare for the most difficult test questions to appear in the retiring topics: Corporate Finance, Quantitative Methods, and Financial Reporting and Analysis. Because these topics will not appear again in Level III, they are at their most difficult in Level II.

- Allocate ample time to large topics such as Equity Investments. Aim for expert proficiency in Financial Reporting and Analysis, as it is both large and being tested for the last time.

- Review Ethics at least four times before test day by working the handbooks into your normal routine every few weeks.

- Study 20 hours per week during the first 14-week study phase in Level II. Finish this initial study phase on time by maintaining a strict weekly schedule and not letting studying scheduled for one week bleed into the next.

- Use the curriculum books extensively in learning the material. Study notes should act as a supporting tool and not as a replacement of the curriculum books.

- Make roughly 600 flashcards as you move through the material, which equates to about 35 flashcards per study session. Avoid squeezing too much information on each one; flashcards are most helpful if they can be reviewed quickly.

- Answer about 900 practice questions during the 14-week study period. This equates to about 50 practice questions per study session. Because the Level II questions are more intricate and may cover multiple concepts, there are typically fewer practice questions for each study session.

- Plan to study 35 hours per week in the last 45 days before test day. During this time, take four practice tests (more if not completely fluent in English or struggling with the Level II material).

- Aim for 75 percent scores on practice tests. Because the Level II minimum passing score (MPS) will likely be 65 percent or lower, this provides a sufficient safety cushion.

- Mind the clock in the Level II exam; candidates typically experience more time pressure than they did in Level I.

Week-by-Week Sample Schedule
Level II

January

MONDAY	TUESDAY	WEDNESDAY	THURSDAY	FRIDAY	SATURDAY	SUNDAY
		1	2	3	4	5
6	7	8	9	10	11	12
13	14	15	16	17	18	19
Ethics (sessions 1 & 2)				Alternative Investments (session 13)		
20	21	22	23	24	25	26
Quantitative Methods (session 3)						
27	28	29	30	31		
Economics (session 4)						

February

MONDAY	TUESDAY	WEDNESDAY	THURSDAY	FRIDAY	SATURDAY	SUNDAY
					1	2
					Economics (session 4)	
3	4	5	6	7	8	9
Corporate Finance (8 & 9)						
10	11	12	13	14	15	16
Financial Reporting and Analysis (5)						
17	18	19	20	21	22	23
Financial Reporting and Analysis (6)						
24	25	26	27	28		
Financial Reporting and Analysis (7)						

March

MONDAY	TUESDAY	WEDNESDAY	THURSDAY	FRIDAY	SATURDAY	SUNDAY
					1	2
					Financial R & A (7)	
3	4	5	6	7	8	9
Equity Investments (10 & 11)						
10	11	12	13	14	15	16
Equity Investments (11)						
17	18	19	20	21	22	23
Fixed Income (14)						
24	25	26	27	28	29	30
Fixed Income (14)				Vacation!		
31						
Vacation!						

April

MONDAY	TUESDAY	WEDNESDAY	THURSDAY	FRIDAY	SATURDAY	SUNDAY
	1	2	3	4	5	6
Derivatives (16)						
7	8	9	10	11	12	13
Derivatives (17)						
14	15	16	17	18	19	20
Portfolio Management (18)						Mock Test 1
21	22	23	24	25	26	27
2nd Review: Alternative Investments			Ethics		Quantitative Methods	
28	29	30				
Quantitative Methods						

May

MONDAY	TUESDAY	WEDNESDAY	THURSDAY	FRIDAY	SATURDAY	SUNDAY
			1	2	3	4
				Economics		Mock 2 Half
5	6	7	8	9	10	11
Corporate Finance		Mock 2 Half	Financial Reporting and Analysis			
12	13	14	15	16	17	18
		Financial Reporting and Analysis				Mock 3 Half
19	20	21	22	23	24	25
Derivatives		Mock 3 Half	Equity Investments			
26	27	28	29	30	31	
Fixed Income			Portfolio Management			

June

MONDAY	TUESDAY	WEDNESDAY	THURSDAY	FRIDAY	SATURDAY	SUNDAY
						1
						Mock Test 4
2	3	4	5	6	7	8
Final Review: Trouble Spots, Ethics, and Flashcards					Test Day!	

LEVEL III RECAP AND SAMPLE SCHEDULE

Key Features of the Level III Exam:

- Ensures mastery of the seven remaining testing topics, with a heavy emphasis on Portfolio Management, which is weighted 45 to 55 percent.

- Gives topic weights in ranges instead of precise weights, with the exception of Ethics, which is weighted 10 percent.

- Offered once per year in June, which means failing candidates must wait a year to repeat the Level.

- Presents "constructed response" questions (essays) in the morning testing session, and multiple-choice questions in vignette format for the afternoon. In answering the essay questions, candidates are not expected to give full sentences or lengthy responses.

Strategies for Passing Level III:

- Study at least 450 hours (500 if not native to the English language). You need time to memorize the curriculum because there will be no answer choices to jog your memory on the essay questions.

- Expect difficult questions in every topic; this exam ensures complete proficiency, so it tends to challenge candidates in all subjects. Make sure to give your weak spots extra attention.

- Review Ethics at least four times before test day, and be sure to review both the *Standards of Practice Handbook* and the additional Level III handbook, *The Asset Manager Code of Professional Conduct.*

- Study 17 hours per week during the first 14-week study phase in Level III. The readings will be shorter than those in Levels I and II, but your understanding of them must be deeper.

- Use the curriculum books extensively in learning the material. Study notes should act as a supporting tool and not as a replacement of the curriculum books.

- Make roughly 450 flashcards as you move through the material, which equates to about 25 flashcards per study session. Make sure to include all lists, definitions, equations, and concepts that could easily become the focus of essay questions.

- Answer as many practice questions as you can, though there are likely to be fewer available than there were in previous Levels. Aim to answer about 700 practice questions during the first 14-week study period, and then study these questions again during your second review period.

- Plan to study 30 hours per week in the last 45 days before test day. Make sure you are comfortable answering essay questions by the end of this period, but don't forget to train for the multiple-choice questions, too.

- Aim for 75 percent scores on practice tests. When grading your exams, be conservative in awarding yourself partial credit.

- Prepare for a significant time crunch on the exam, particularly in the essay session. If you lack a native's command of the English language, consider completing practice tests in five hours instead of six to train for the time pressure.

Week-by-Week Sample Schedule
Level III

January

MONDAY	TUESDAY	WEDNESDAY	THURSDAY	FRIDAY	SATURDAY	SUNDAY
		1	2	3	4	5
6	7	8	9	10	11	12
13	14	15	16	17	18	19
Portfolio Management: Behavioral Finance (session 3)						
20	21	22	23	24	25	26
Ethics (sessions 1 & 2)						
27	28	29	30	31		
Portfolio Management: Individual (session 4)						

February

MONDAY	TUESDAY	WEDNESDAY	THURSDAY	FRIDAY	SATURDAY	SUNDAY
					1	2
					Port. Management (session 4)	
3	4	5	6	7	8	9
Portfolio Management: Institutional (5)						
10	11	12	13	14	15	16
Portfolio Management: Capital Markets (6)				Portfolio Management: Economics (7)		
17	18	19	20	21	22	23
Portfolio Management: Asset Allocation (8)				Fixed Income (9)		
24	25	26	27	28		
Fixed Income (9)						

March

MONDAY	TUESDAY	WEDNESDAY	THURSDAY	FRIDAY	SATURDAY	SUNDAY
					1	2
					Derivatives (10)	
3	4	5	6	7	8	9
Equity Investments (11 & 12)						
10	11	12	13	14	15	16
Alternative Investments (13)				Portfolio Management: Risk (14)		
17	18	19	20	21	22	23
Portfolio Management: Risk (14)						
24	25	26	27	28	29	30
Portfolio Management: Risk (15)				Vacation!		
31						
Vacation!						

April

MONDAY	TUESDAY	WEDNESDAY	THURSDAY	FRIDAY	SATURDAY	SUNDAY
	1	2	3	4	5	6
	Portfolio Management: Trading (16)					
7	8	9	10	11	12	13
Portfolio Management: Performance Evaluation (17)					Portfolio Management: GIPS	
14	15	16	17	18	19	20
Portfolio Management: Global Investment Performance Standards (18)						Mock Test 1
21	22	23	24	25	26	27
2nd Review: Behavioral		Portfolio Management: Individual				Ethics
28	29	30				
Portfolio Management: Institutional						

May

MONDAY	TUESDAY	WEDNESDAY	THURSDAY	FRIDAY	SATURDAY	SUNDAY
			1	2	3	4
			Portfolio Management: Capital Markets			Mock 2 Half
5	6	7	8	9	10	11
Port Mgmt: Economics		Mock 2 Half	Port Mgmt: Asset Allocation		Fixed Income	
12	13	14	15	16	17	18
Equity Investments				Derivatives	Alternative	Mock 3 Half
19	20	21	22	23	24	25
Port Mgmt: Performance Eval		Mock 3 Half	Portfolio Management: Risk			
26	27	28	29	30	31	
Portfolio Management: Trading, Portfolio Management				GIPS		

June

MONDAY	TUESDAY	WEDNESDAY	THURSDAY	FRIDAY	SATURDAY	SUNDAY
						1
						Mock Test 4
2	3	4	5	6	7	8
Final Review: Trouble Spots, Ethics, and Flashcards					Test Day!	

TEST PREPARATION RESOURCES

There are various resources available to the CFA candidate in every Level, including discussion forums, study systems, and classes. I've listed many of these resources below and starred the ones that I used in passing my exams. This doesn't mean the rest are not worth checking out. Some are new and if had been available, I would have benefited from them. Others didn't entice me, but may be perfect for you. I recommend looking into all of these resource options before choosing and laying out a study plan.

Study Systems

- **Allen Resources:** Offers all the standard tools expected in a study system, plus extras like video lectures. Candidates can sign up for an affordable month-to-month subscription that can be cancelled any time. Additionally, Allen Resources ranks your performance on groups of practice questions against other candidates.

★ **AnalystNotes:** Provides online study notes, practice questions, review quizzes, and practice tests for Levels I and II (not Level III). AnalystNotes is one of the most economical choices available. Your performance on each AnalystNotes practice test is benchmarked against all other candidates taking the same test.

• **BPP University:** Offers a convenient and helpful preview of its study materials so you can make an informed decision. With customizable packages, you can easily design a study package that fits your needs with reasonable prices.

★ **CFA Institute Curriculum:** Yields every test question and the answers, so these books are critical to any study plan. Even in Level I, which lends itself to using study notes more heavily, the curriculum books provide practice questions and example problems that are important in every Level.

• **Elan Guides:** Offers both pre-designed packages (study notes, mock exams, video lectures, etc.) and highly customizable packages which let you pay for only what you need and nothing else.

• **Fitch Learning:** Offers the full CFA-test prep gamut including study notes, practice questions, video lectures, mock exams, mobile applications, webinars, and more, though Fitch Learning is one of the priciest options.

★ **Kaplan Schweser:** Known as a full-service provider with all the trimmings, Kaplan Schweser is a popular but expensive choice.

Test Preparation Classes

- **BPP University:** A London-based provider that holds live classes in several United Kingdom cities at different times to help you find an option that fits your schedule.

- **Fitch Learning:** Providing live classes in New York City in the United States and Toronto in Canada on weekends and evenings.

- **Kaplan Schweser:** Offers in-person classes in seven cities in the United States, plus opportunities in 34 other worldwide locations across six continents through Kaplan Schweser's partners. Kaplan Schweser also holds weekly online classes in both London and U.S. Eastern time that simulate the live class experience for anyone not interested in or able to attend the live version.

- **Local, Independent CFA Mentors:** In many cities, a CFA charterholder or higher-Level candidate will assist a group of candidates in preparing for the CFA exams, or he or she may tutor candidates one-on-one. Search in your city to see if this option is available.

- **Your Local CFA Society:** Some CFA societies hold weekly, in-person classes that are taught by CFA charterholders and begin a few months before the exam. However, these are often only offered for Level I.

Online Discussion Forums

- **300Hours.com:** A newer forum moderated by CFA charterholders, plus regularly updated blogs written by charterholders and forum members.

★ **AnalystForum.com:** A well-established forum that, at the time of this writing, had 805,017 total user posts on 80,832 CFA topics. If you have a question on the CFA Program, it's probably been asked and answered here.

• **Forum.CFAspace.com:** Another highly visited forum site with easy navigation between Levels and major topic areas (Ethics, Investment Tools, Portfolio Management, and Asset Valuation).

• **Thomson Reuters Messenger:** A unique option that offers live question-and-answer chat room sessions with CFA tutors on a weekly basis at no cost. Partners with Fitch Learning, which offers study systems and test prep classes (see above).

ABOUT THE AUTHOR

Rachel Bryant is a CFA charterholder who passed each of the Chartered Financial Analyst exams on her first try within two consecutive years. She is a risk manager for a large banking organization in the southeastern United States, which lets her apply her CFA training on a daily basis. Her work focuses on supervising the market, liquidity, and capital risks of the largest banks in the world.

In addition to the CFA charter, Rachel also holds the Professional Risk Manager (PRM) designation and takes any opportunity to further her financial and overall knowledge. Rachel earned her bachelor's degree from the Georgia Institute of Technology (GA Tech) with a concentration in Finance.

Though her banking work keeps her busy, Rachel enjoys writing in her spare time. Known for her honest, direct style, Rachel is an internationally published author on risk management and financial topics. She brings a unique perspective to the risk management industry, and is regularly featured in trade journals such as *Intelligent Risk*. Rachel also writes on career-related topics, including the CFA Program, and blogs at www.TheCareerCohort.com.

Rachel's working life is important, but her most significant and cherished role is that of devoted wife, daughter, sister, and friend. She loves to travel, backpack in the great outdoors, and help keep up her family's small farm. Rachel is thankful for many things, but above all her caring family and friends. She hopes to make them proud.

Rachel is a guest contributor to financial publications. For availability, please email her at rachel@rachel-bryant.com. Learn more about Rachel at www.Rachel-Bryant.com.

REFERENCES

[1] CFA Institute. (2013). Candidate examination results. Retrieved from http://www.cfainstitute.org/programs/cfaprogram/Documents/1963_current_candidate_exam_results.pdf

[2] CFA Institute. (2013, November 5). CFA charters earned worldwide. Retrieved from http://www.cfainstitute.org/programs/cfaprogram/charter/map/pages/index.aspx.
CFA Institute. (2013). Candidate examination results. Retrieved from http://www.cfainstitute.org/programs/cfaprogram/Documents/1963_current_candidate_exam_results.pdf

[3] CFA Institute. (n.d.). CFA exam fee schedule. Retrieved from http://www.cfainstitute.org/programs/cfaprogram/register/Pages/fee_schedule.aspx

[4] CFA Institute. (n.d.). Candidate body of knowledge topic outline. Retrieved from http://www.cfainstitute.org/programs/cfaprogram/courseofstudy/Pages/cbok.aspx

[5] CFA Institute, 2012. *Prep Provider Guidelines Program Manual.* Charlottesville, VA: CFA Institute.

[6] CFA Institute. (n.d.). LOS command words [manual]. Retrieved from http://www.cfainstitute.org/programs/Documents/cfa_and_cipm_los_command_words.pdf

[7] CFA Institute. (n.d.). Work experience guidelines. Retrieved from http://www.cfainstitute.org/community/membership/process/Pages/work_experience.aspx?PageName=searchresults&ResultsPage=1

[8] CFA Institute. (n.d.). Research and data. Retrieved from http://www.cfainstitute.org/about/research/Pages/index.aspx

[9] CFA Institute. (n.d.). Exam details. Retrieved from http://www.cfainstitute.org/programs/cfaprogram/exams/Pages/index.aspx

[10] CFA Institute. (2013, November 5). CFA charters earned worldwide. Retrieved from http://www.cfainstitute.org/programs/cfaprogram/charter/map/pages/index.aspx

[11] CFA Institute. (2013-2014). CFA exam topic area weights. Retrieved from http://www.cfainstitute.org/programs/cfaprogram/exams/Pages/exam_topic_area_weights.aspx

[12] CFA Society of Chicago (as cited by CFA Society of Minnesota, 2013). (n.d.). CFA exam tips and reminders. Retrieved from http://www.cfasociety.org/minnesota/Pages/CFA_Exam_Tips.aspx

[13] Johnson, R. R., Lamy, B., Mackey, P. B., & Squires, J. R. (n.d.). *The CFA Program: Our Fifth Decade*. Charlottesville, VA: CFA Institute.

[14] CFA Institute. (n.d.). Tips for taking the CFA Exam. Retrieved from http://www.cfainstitute.org/programs/cfaprogram/exams/Pages/tips_for_taking_exam.aspx?PageName=searchresults&ResultsPage=1

[15] CFA Institute. (February 4, 2011). *Standards of Practice Handbook* (10th ed.). Charlottesville, VA.

[16] CFA Institute. (n.d.). Exam-related disciplinary actions. Retrieved from http://www.cfainstitute.org/ethics/conduct/sanctions/Pages/candidate_sanctions.aspx

[17] CFA Institute. (2013). Candidate examination results. Retrieved from http://www.cfainstitute.org/programs/cfaprogram/Documents/1963_current_candidate_exam_results.pdf

[18] CFA Institute. (2013). Candidate examination results. Retrieved from http://www.cfainstitute.org/programs/cfaprogram/Documents/196 3_current_candidate_exam_results.pdf

[19] CFA Institute. 2013. June 2013 CFA® program candidate survey report. Retrieved from http://www.cfainstitute.org/Survey/candidate_survey_2013.pdf

[20] CFA Institute. (2012). *Prep Provider Guidelines Program Manual.* Charlottesville, VA: CFA Institute.

[21] Johnson, R. R., Lamy, B., Mackey, P. B., & Squires, J. R. (n.d.). *The CFA Program: Our Fifth Decade.* Charlottesville, VA: CFA Institute.

[22] CFA Institute. (n.d.) CFA program testing policies. Retrieved from http://www.cfainstitute.org/programs/cfaprogram/exams/Pages/poli cies.aspx